# AMERICAN TROUBLEMAKERS

## John Brown: Militant Abolitionist

# T★★AMERICAN★★S TROUBLEMAKERS

# JOHN BROWN:
## Militant Abolitionist

Robert R. Potter

With an Introduction by James P. Shenton

RSVP
RAINTREE
STECK-VAUGHN
P U B L I S H E R S
The Steck-Vaughn Company

Austin, Texas

**CONSULTANTS**

Richard M. Haynes
Director, Office of Field
   Experiences and Certification
College of Education and Psychology
Western Carolina University
Cullowhee, North Carolina

Catherine J. Lenix-Hooker
Executive Director
Krueger-Scott Mansion Cultural
   Center
Newark, New Jersey

**MANAGING EDITOR**
Richard G. Gallin

**PROJECT MANAGER**
Julie Klaus

**PHOTO EDITOR**
Margie Foster

*A Gallin House Press Book*

**Library of Congress Cataloging-in-Publication Data**
Potter, Robert R. (Robert Russell)
    John Brown: militant abolitionist/Robert R. Potter; with an introduction by James P. Shenton.
       p.   cm. — (American Troublemakers)
    "A Gallin House Press Book."
    Includes bibliographical references ( p.  ) and index.
    ISBN 0-8114-2378-6
    1. Brown, John, 1800-1859 — Juvenile literature.   2. Abolitionists — United States — Biography — Juvenile literature.   [1. Brown, John, 1800-1859.   2. Abolitionists.]   I.Title.   II. Series.
E451.P78   1995
973.7'116'092—dc20
[B]                                   94-17020
                                         CIP
                                         AC

Printed and bound in the United States.
1 2 3 4 5 6 7 8 9 0  LB  99 98 97 96 95 94

# CONTENTS

John Brown

# INTRODUCTION

### by James P. Shenton

Biography is the history of the individual lives of men and women. In all lives, there is a sequence that begins with birth, evolves into the development of character in childhood and adolescence, is followed by the emergence of maturity in adulthood, and finally concludes with death. All lives follow this pattern, although with each emerge the differences that make each life unique. These distinctive characteristics are usually determined by the particular area in which a person has been most active. An artist draws his or her specific identity from the area of the arts in which he or she has been most active. So the writer becomes an author; the musician, a performer or composer; the politician, a senator, governor, president, or statesperson. The intellectual discipline to which one is attached identifies the scientist, historian, economist, literary critic, or political scientist, among many. Some aspects of human behavior are identified as heroic, cowardly, corrupt, or just ordinary. The task of the biographer is to explain why a particular life is worth remembering. And if the effort is successful, the reader draws from it insights into a vast range of behavior patterns. In a sense, biography provides lessons from life.

Some lives become important because of the position a person holds. Typical would be that of a U.S. President in which a biographer compares the various incumbents to determine their comparative importance. Without question, Abraham Lincoln was a profoundly significant President, much more so than Warren G. Harding whose administration was swamped by corruption. Others achieve importance because of their role in a particular area. So Emily Dickinson and Carl Sandburg are recognized as important poets and Albert Einstein as a great scientist.

Implicit in the choice of biographical subjects is the idea that each somehow affected history. Their lives explain something about the world in which they lived, even as they affect our lives and those of generations to come. But there is another consideration: Some lives are more interesting than those of others. Within each life is a great story that illuminates human behavior.

7

Then there are those people who are troublemakers, people whom we cannot ignore. They are the people who both upset and fascinate us. Their singular quality is that they are uniquely different. Troublemakers are irritating, perhaps frightening, frustrating, and disturbing, but never dull. They march to their own drummer and they are original.

John Brown is impossible to imagine in any country other than the United States. Those who knew him compared him to the rock-ribbed land of his native Puritan New England. Some surviving portraits depict a man who looks like a biblical prophet. The core of Brown's beliefs was derived from the Old Testament. The God to whom he prayed was the Father whose justice was at the heart of all things. John Brown demanded from all believers a rigorous commitment to the word of God. Compromise had no place in his thought.

Nothing was more important to John Brown than his unswerving opposition to and hatred of slavery. For him, true abolitionism meant a willingness to share with enslaved people the dangers of their condition. It meant reaching out to fugitive slaves and aiding them to escape their enslavement. It also meant a willingness to enter the Southern home of slavery and attempt to lead a slave rebellion. The fact that the U.S. Constitution acknowledged the legality of slavery meant for Brown that the Constitution was a "compact with Hell." God's justice demanded unrelenting opposition to the existence of slavery. His whole life underscored that commitment.

John Brown's consistent message on slavery was that it would not go away peacefully and, therefore, abolitionists had to embrace violence. As John Brown explained at the trial where he was condemned to death for leading the attack on Harper's Ferry, blood alone would purge America of the sin of slavery, and violent opposition to slavery would do more for abolitionism than a thousand years of peaceful agitation. Within less than two years of John Brown's execution, a generation of Americans marched off to the Civil War. It took the deaths of more than 600,000 other Americans, before John Brown's goal of ending slavery was achieved.

# CHAPTER ONE

## "Not Much of a Schollar"

John Brown was the man who, in October 1859, struck the first blow in what became the Civil War. With a self-styled "army" of 21 men, he raided a government weapons center at Harper's Ferry, Virginia (now Harpers Ferry, West Virginia). The raid failed in its purpose, to free the enslaved people whom Brown thought would come running to his banner. John Brown was captured. Six weeks later he was hanged for murder and treason.

But in another sense, John Brown's famous raid won him what he wanted. He was a God-fearing man who believed with a

John Brown was born in this farmhouse in Torrington in northwestern Connecticut, 17 years after the end of the Revolutionary War.

passion that all people are created equal. He took the Golden Rule as a law of life: He should do unto others as he would have others do unto him. He thought of himself as a kind of modern-day Moses, chosen by God to lead 4 million African Americans out of bondage. Better for the whole land to be bathed in blood, he told people, than for slavery to continue even one more day. That wish came true less than two years after his death, as both South and North rose up to fight the bloodiest war in American history.

When John Brown is mentioned, people usually think first of his fabled death: the *body* that lies a-moldering in the grave, the *soul* that marches on. But the John Brown behind the legend was just as human as anyone who ever lived. His 59 years of living are what give his death a special meaning.

John Brown's name is among the most famous in American history. His life is certainly one of the most argued about. This book is the story of that life.

John Brown was born on May 9, 1800, on a rocky hillside farm in Torrington, Connecticut. At that time, the United States of America was only 11 years old. The young nation was made up of the 13 original colonies, plus Vermont, Kentucky, and Tennessee. Inventions such as the railroad and the telegraph were years in the future. Most American families scratched out a poor living on small farms. Life was hard.

John Brown's parents, Owen and Ruth Brown, were just such a family. Owen's life had been an uphill struggle. When Owen was five, his father—also named John Brown—had died in George Washington's army during the American Revolution. The dead soldier's large, penniless family had to shift for itself on a tiny Connecticut farm. Everyone worked. Everyone also went hungry at times. One spring a neighbor gave the family the service of a strong black slave for a few days to help with the plowing. (Slavery was legal in Connecticut until after the Revolution.) At times the slave would carry little Owen around on his broad back. The kindness and character of this African American left a mark on young Owen. All his life he hated slavery.

When Owen was 12, he went to work for a cobbler, or shoe-maker. He also learned the skill of tanning animal hides. Then, at

Owen Brown, John Brown's deeply religious father, ran a farm and tannery in Connecticut before the family moved to Ohio.

19, he became a "born-again" Christian. He married Ruth Mills, who was a minister's daughter. When their first two babies died, Owen wondered what sin of the parents had prompted the Lord to act in God's mysterious way. The sin of pride, he thought. After all, he had started with nothing, and now he couldn't help feeling proud of his farm, his tannery, and his cobbler's shop. Owen was a man whose mild, humble manner hid high-minded honor and a great inner strength.

When John Brown was four, his father began to think that he

had done about as much as he could on the Torrington farm. The Connecticut hills offered few new customers for his shoes and his hides. At the time, more than a few Connecticut families were pulling up stakes and moving to eastern Ohio. In the summer of 1804, Owen Brown went to have a look at this new frontier. He liked what he saw. He liked it so much that he bought some wooded acres and started building a small cabin before he returned to Connecticut.

In 1805, when John was five, the family made the long trip to their new home in Hudson, Ohio. They made quite a picture as they started west on the dusty road that ran past the two-story Brown farmhouse. First went Owen, walking beside the team of oxen that pulled the creaking farm wagon. In the wagon were Ruth and three of the children, as well as all the family's belongings. Their small herd of cattle came next, followed by John and an older brother on horses.

Of course little John was thrilled. He was going to "a wilderness filled with wild beasts, & Indians," as he later put it. Soon they dropped out of the Connecticut hills onto the open land of New York State. Every turn in the road, every new view, had its own special tingle. They crossed the broad Hudson River on a ferry. In the evenings, as the animals grazed, there was a campfire, and then a sound sleep beneath a star-studded sky. Pennsylvania seemed like one mountain range after another—up and down, up and down. John worried some about the first Native Americans he saw and also about the "Rattle Snakes which were very large." But at last they reached Pittsburgh. Then, after more mountains, they reached the fertile land around Hudson, Ohio. The trip took 48 days.

At first, life in Ohio was far from easy. Owen Brown had only an axe and his own hardened muscles to turn forestland into fields. The cabin was cold and much too small for a family of seven. The first winter, the Browns lived largely on the kindness of neighbors and what deer and wild turkeys could be shot in the woods. They also fed on Owen's vision of a better life come spring.

Years later, at the age of 57, John Brown wrote a short account of his early years in Hudson. He remembered himself as an active boy who "might generally be seen *barefooted,* & *bareheaded*: with Buckskin Breeches suspended often with one leather strap over his shoulder but sometimes with Two." There were many Native Americans around Hudson, and John was fascinated with them. He "used to hang about them quite as much as was consistent with good manners & learned a trifle of their talk." He had "but little chance of going to school at all," although he was for a short time sent to school. He loved "the *hardest & roughest* kinds of plays" with other boys. Work in his father's tannery pleased him more than the schoolroom. He admitted that he was "not . . . much of a schollar" (and note that the last word is misspelled).

Many of John Brown's earliest memories concerned heart-breaking losses. As a boy on a frontier farm, his "earthly treasures were very *few & small*." When he lost one of these few treasures, it often "*took years to heal the wound*." When he was six, a Native American friend about his age gave him a small, round yellow stone, a marble, the first such object he had ever seen. John valued it beyond price. When it strangely vanished, he "cried at times about it." Soon after he caught a young squirrel, tearing off its tail in the process. But he managed to tame little Bob Tail. It became a household pet. Its disappearance left John "*in mourning*" for years. Later his father gave him a cuddly little lamb to raise as his own. Its sickness and death left an aching space in its young owner.

But these losses were as nothing compared with the death of Ruth Brown in 1808. John's mother died in childbirth, and the baby also died. Such double deaths were not uncommon at the time. Owen Brown, left alone with the children (one of whom the Browns had recently adopted), was crushed. "This sean all most makes my heart blead now," he wrote years later. Owen remarried the following year, but John could never accept Sally Root Brown as any kind of a mother. Friends at the time said that John became even more rough-and-tumble in his ways. John Brown never wrote much about his stepmother, perhaps because he had little good to say. What little is known about Sally Brown comes from other sources. One account—which may or may not be true—claims that John and his brother once made a crude bomb triggered to blow up Sally Brown when she was in the outhouse. Fortunately for the poor woman, the device failed to go off.

It is true, however, that at about the age of 10 John was introduced to the study of history. A well-educated man in Hudson took an interest in the boy and gave him free use of his library. John grew to admire "the lives of great, wise & good men and their sayings, & writings." He also preferred the company of older men whom he considered wise and good. At the same time he developed a dislike for small talk—and for people with small minds. He considered the reading of novels a waste of time. He would never learn to dance or to play cards. Hunting and fishing, he thought, were excuses for idleness.

In the busy Brown barns and tannery, there was much to do. Owen Brown was a man with an eye for every chance. On the side he bought and sold cattle. Young John liked helping his father on cattle drives. These trips sometimes took them away from home for days at a time. By the age of 12, John was considered man enough to go on these drives himself. During the War of 1812, he drove a small herd more than 100 miles to provide beef for an American army stationed near Detroit, Michigan Territory.

It was at this time in his life that John Brown got his first real look at slavery, American style. Far from Hudson, he wrote years later, he stayed for a short time in the home of a well-fixed gentleman, a person of some importance. One of the servants was an African American boy about John's age. The slave and the stranger soon became friends. John was horrified at the way the enslaved boy was treated. At mealtime, the gentleman seated John near him and showered him with attention. Yet the black boy, waiting on table, was treated with utter contempt. At the slightest excuse, the master would beat the slave "with Iron Shovels or any other thing that first came to hand." The slave boy was poorly clothed, poorly fed, and forced to sleep in the cold. John was sickened by "the wretched, hopeless condition of *Fatherless* & *Motherless* slave children." "Is God their Father?" he sometimes asked himself.

Back in Hudson, John put all his energies into the family tanning business, which continued to do well. As Owen Brown added more workers, his son John gradually took over as foreman. The 15-year-old tannery boss insisted that everything be done exactly in the right way. John found that he enjoyed giving orders—and seeing them obeyed. This new-found power over other people both pleased and puzzled him. "There was such force and mastery in what he did," a neighbor later remembered, "that everything gave way before him." One of John's younger brothers called him "a King against whom there is no rising up." Even John wondered if he wasn't getting too used to bossing others around. He, himself, could not easily take orders or even listen to other people.

John did, however, listen closely to the call of God that he felt in his heart during his 16th year. It was more than a "born-again" experience. He quite suddenly decided to become a minister. No matter that he had almost no education at all. No matter that he lived far from the center of things. John felt that God had chosen him to preach the gospel. He had no other choice. It was as simple as that.

Owen Brown agreed. He would lose a good foreman but at the same time would add a willing soldier to God's great army on earth. The beginning step would be for John to graduate from a good college in the East. John chose Amherst College in Massachusetts. To get into college, however, he would first have to attend an academy, as the high schools of that time were called.

Late in 1816, John Brown left Hudson, Ohio, for Plainfield Academy in Plainfield, Massachusetts. One story says that Owen Brown let him take two horses and some good sheepskins to pay his bills. Already John was the eager Bible reader who would soon know much of that long book by heart.

Things did not go well at Plainfield. One reason, probably, was John Brown's difference from the other students. He was 16, but his weathered face and adult manner made him seem 20 or more. His thin, hawklike nose; his steely blue-gray eyes; his close-cut crop of brown hair brushed straight back; his ramrod posture—all made him look like a frontier soldier, not a student. And here he sat beside youths of 12 and 14, many of them from upper-class Eastern homes. It made things worse that his fellow students already knew more about Latin, Greek, grammar, and mathematics than John could learn for some time.

15

John Brown briefly attended Morris Academy in Litchfield, Connecticut, a few miles south of where he had been born.

After a few months, John Brown transferred to Morris Academy in Litchfield, Connecticut. But the move made little difference. He *did* try, pouring over his books night after night by the light of lanterns and flickering candles. Perhaps he tried too hard. His eyes grew red to the point of pain. Before long he could not bear to read at all. Also, it grew clear that the coming years of study would cost more than his father could afford. In 1817, he gave up the struggle and headed back to Hudson.

It was the first of John Brown's many failures.

# CHAPTER TWO

## Man of Many Missions

In John Brown's day, the tanning of hides was hard and messy work. Sheepskins were handled in one piece; cowhides were cut in two to begin the process. First, all traces of blood, flesh, and other soft matter had to be scraped off with a special knife. After this "beaming," sheepskins were watered down in piles to "sweat" until the hair could be removed. Cowhides were soaked in a strong solution of lye to loosen the hair. Then, the hides were placed in huge vats between layers of ground-up bark, to soak for a long time. Last, the skins were hung on poles to dry. Other processes could make lambskins soft enough for dainty gloves, cowhides stiff enough for saddles.

It was to such work in his father's tannery that John Brown returned when he gave up on a minister's career in 1817. He

As a teenager, John Brown worked in his father's tannery, similar to this one, converting animal hides into leather.

tanned not only the skins of cattle and sheep, calves and lambs, but also deerskins for "Buckskin Breeches." He boasted that he could also handle "leather such as Squirrel, Raccoon, Cat, Wolf, or Dog Skins," and once again, the bossy foreman "doted on being head of the heap," as a neighbor put it.

In fact, after about a year the young tanner was no longer happy with his job as his father's foreman. He wanted to be head of his *own* heap. With his brother Levi, Brown built a new tannery about a mile from Hudson, on the road to Cleveland. The Brown brothers kept "Bachelors hall" in a nearby cabin. John baked the bread and did the cooking. In his kitchen, as in everything, he had to be neat and clean. That was John Brown's way. He was a strangely serious and somber young man who had almost no social life. Instead, he devoted long days to "close attention to *business*; & success in its management." Somehow he also found time to upgrade his arithmetic, and he even taught himself surveying, no easy task. He would work as a surveyor now and then for the rest of his life.

Brown's "close attention" paid off, and the business expanded. To work for John Brown was an experience not everyone enjoyed, but no one ever forgot. He insisted that all employees go to church on Sunday. Every working day began with Bible readings followed by prayer. Brown was a harsh taskmaster. He put up with no second best.

As the business grew, the Browns' cabin was enlarged to accommodate the workers who wished to board with their employer. By and by, it made little sense for John Brown to do the baking and cooking. He hired a widow named Mary Lusk to take over the household work. Before long her 18-year-old daughter, Dianthe, was added to the staff. Dianthe was a small, sweet girl whose singing voice added a bright new meaning to Brown's favorite hymns. She was cheerful, but never funny; competent, but never challenging. One of her favorite free-time activities was to go to a secret place in the woods and pray to God.

John Brown and Dianthe Lusk were married on June 21, 1820. He was 20, and she was 19. In his short account of his early years, Brown later praised Dianthe for being "*remarkably plain.*" The no-nonsense tanner who valued plainness in all things now had

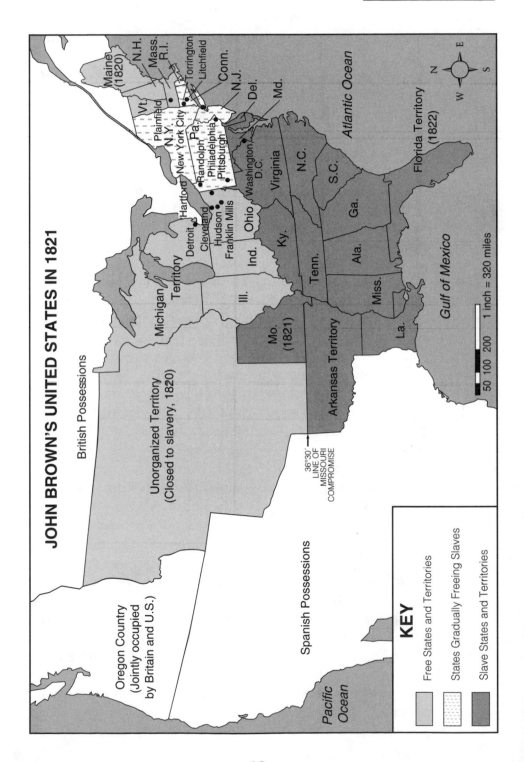

# JOHN BROWN'S UNITED STATES IN 1821

British Possessions

Oregon Country
(Jointly occupied
by Britain and U.S.)

Unorganized Territory
(Closed to slavery, 1820)

Spanish Possessions

Pacific
Ocean

Michigan
Territory

Ill.

Ind.

Ohio

Mo.
(1821)

Arkansas Territory

36°30'
LINE OF
MISSOURI
COMPROMISE

Detroit
Cleveland
Hudson
Franklin Mills

Hartford

Maine
(1820)

Vt.

N.H.

Mass.

R.I.

Conn.

Torrington
Litchfield

Plainfield

N.Y.

New York City

N.J.

Del.

Pa.

Pittsburgh

Randolph
Philadelphia

Md.

Washington,
D.C.

Virginia

Ky.

Tenn.

N.C.

S.C.

Ga.

Ala.

Miss.

La.

Florida Territory
(1822)

Atlantic Ocean

Gulf of Mexico

N
W      E
S

1 inch = 320 miles

50  100  200

## KEY

Free States and Territories

States Gradually Freeing Slaves

Slave States and Territories

19

just the wife he wanted. Their first child, John Brown Jr., was born about a year later. More children followed, and with them a new white-clapboard house. The new home, with its surrounding orchard and garden, spoke silently of its young owner's success.

It has always been something of a mystery why John Brown decided quite suddenly in 1825 to leave Hudson, Ohio, for the wilds around Randolph, Pennsylvania. For its time and location, Hudson was a good place to live. It was a town of some culture, already known as an antislavery center. A college, Western Reserve, was being founded in Hudson just as John Brown left the town.

One reason for the move was probably the old Brown family urge to pull up stakes and try life somewhere else. Twenty years before, Owen Brown had done the same thing. Now his son John would also move to the wilderness, clear land, and raise his young family in a growing community. Also, although little about her is known, Dianthe was never a strong person, in body or in mind. John Brown may have thought she would be happier in fresh surroundings. Finally, the simple fact was that the right kinds of bark for Brown's tannery were growing scarce around Hudson. Instead of hauling bark great distances, Brown thought, why not haul the hides to where hemlock and oak trees grew in abundance?

The town of Randolph, not too far from Hudson across the Pennsylvania line, no longer exists. It was 12 miles from modern-day Meadville. At the time it was wild country. Not only deer and turkeys, but bears and wolves prowled the woods. Nevertheless, the oaks were there, the hemlocks were there, and land sold for next to nothing. Brown bought 200 acres, then returned to Hudson for his wife and three little boys. He would be the first businessman, and almost the first farmer, to move into town.

John Brown's activity during his first Randolph year staggered all who saw it. He cleared 25 acres, chopping down trees and prying huge rocks from the soil. The rocks became the foundation and lower walls of a large 18-vat tannery. Some of the trees became a log house. It had two large downstairs rooms with a huge fireplace on each end. He also built a barn that contained a secret room to hide runaway slaves. By the fall of 1826, the tannery was in full operation and employed at least 10 men. Seth Thompson, a business partner in Hudson, Ohio, was regularly sending Brown hides to tan at a profit.

At this time, too, John Brown turned his attention to breeding "fine Cattle, Horses, Sheep; & Swine." He paid good money for foundation stock, and his Saxony sheep and Devon cattle were soon winning honors at country fairs. Brown had a great way with animals. He began to believe that he had been born a shepherd at heart.

Once his own home base was established, Brown reached out to do what he could for the community. He started a school, and because there were no real teaching requirements except the ability to read and do simple arithmetic, he even taught now and then. He organized a church, in which he sometimes preached. (Since the Bible was *the* great book for Brown, a guide to life and a source of salvation, there was often little difference between his teaching and his preaching.) He helped get a post office for the town and served as postmaster for seven years. Brown even surveyed roads and properties.

As in Hudson, Brown considered himself a self-appointed "brother's keeper." When he met a new person in the community, he would skip the small talk and get right to the two key questions: Did the newcomer observe the Sabbath, and did he or she agree that human slavery was an abomination in the eyes of God? The right answers earned the newcomer acceptance, the wrong answers Brown's scorn.

A similar high-minded authority can be seen in Brown's own home. "He commanded," a son wrote later, "and there was obedience." All the Brown children later remembered their father's whippings. A strange and telling story comes from John Brown Jr.

Old enough to work but inclined to be lazy at times—or to rebel against John Brown's long hours—John Jr. built up a list of punishments in what he called his father's "book-account":

> John, Jr.,
>
> | | |
> |---|---|
> | For disobeying mother | 8 lashes |
> | For unfaithfulness at work | 3 lashes |
> | For telling a lie | 8 lashes |

One Sunday morning, John Jr. states, his father decided that "it was time for a settlement." With a beechwood switch in hand, father John took son John to the tannery. (John Brown was never known for his puns—but who knows?) John Jr. bared his back and prepared for the worst. The cruel whip lashed down. Its quick, hot touches made the boy's every nerve leap and shudder. John Jr. counted the blows. After receiving about a third of his punishment, "to my utter astonishment, father stripped off his shirt, and, seating himself on the block, gave me the whip and bade me 'lay it on' to his bare back. I dared not refuse to obey, but at first I did not strike hard."

"Harder!" commanded the older John Brown.

"Harder! Harder!"

The boy raised the whip and lashed down again and again, until his father "received the balance of the account. Small drops of blood showed on his back where the tip end of the tingling beech cut through. Thus ended the account and settlement, which was also my first practical illustration of the Doctrine of the Atonement."

According to this doctrine, God is most pleased when the innocent volunteer to suffer along with the guilty for sins against divine law, as set forth in the Bible. Why should the innocent suffer? Because they, as members of the human family, are responsible for that family's living up to God's laws. John Brown believed that Jesus Christ had taken on the sins of humanity and suffered therefor. In much the same way, Christ's servant John Brown could take on the sins of his beloved children and then share the suffering necessary to relieve the crushing burden of sin.

Although the Brown children remembered the whippings, they also remembered the tears that flowed from their father's eyes as the lash descended. In Brown's view, the children had not simply disobeyed an order from father or mother. No, they had disobeyed a law of God. Every word in the Bible carried divine truth, and God's laws of conduct were clearly set forth in the Old Testament. All human beings, John Brown included, were born in sin and deserved divine punishment. (Brown's letters are full of comments on his "unworthy" nature that is again "smarting under the rod of our Heavenly Father.") In trying to lead a child away from sinful ways, Brown believed, a father who whipped a child was doing his obedient best to carry out God's purposes.

Whipping children for misdeeds was much more common in that day than this. Like most boys and girls at the time, the young Browns expected to be whipped. And in most cases, John Brown's children believed his punishment of them fit the crime. Jason Brown, the second oldest son and a mild, gentle person by nature, remembered being whipped only twice. His younger sister Ruth, more lively and headstrong, later admitted that she was whipped only once when she really didn't deserve it.

If John Brown was often hard on others, he was even harder on himself. He considered it his duty to stay up all night with a sick child so that Dianthe could get her rest. Every morning he was up with or before the sun. He lived to work hard; a moment wasted was a moment lost. He dressed simply. He permitted himself no luxuries like coffee or tobacco. An example of Brown's struggle to gain mastery over himself was later reported by one of his younger sons, Salmon Brown.

About 1830, John Brown was to help in a local barn raising. (A barn raising was a party to help a neighbor erect precut beams into the frame of a barn.) Wanting some liquor for the occasion, the owner of the barn-to-be gave Brown 75 cents to purchase a three-gallon jug of whiskey in Meadville. John Brown "was accustomed to drinking from his own barrel," Salmon Brown states, "and did not think the practice wrong." But between Meadville and the barn raising, "father became thirsty and began taking 'nips' from the jug." Soon John Brown "realized that liquor was getting hold of him, and he became alarmed. . . . He reasoned that if the liquor would lead him to drink from another man's jug it was surely gaining control over him—a thing he could not allow. Coming to a large rock by the roadway, he smashed the jug upon it, vowing that he would not be responsible for his neighbor's drinking at the barn-raising, where accidents might happen. He paid for the liquor, and when he reached home rolled his whisky barrel into the back yard and smashed it to pieces with an ax. No liquor was allowed about the house afterwards."

Many of the children's memories of John Brown can be summed up in three words: *concern for others.* A group of Native

An 1817 print depicting an African American being beaten.
Brown proclaimed that enslaving people was morally wrong.

Americans from New York State liked to winter in the woods around Randolph, where game was plentiful. When some of his neighbors wanted to take up arms and drive the Native Americans out, Brown insisted on their right to hunt where they wanted in their own country.

But it was American slavery that really brought force to Brown's steely eyes and wide, stubborn jaw. He continued to feed, clothe, and hide runaway slaves making their way to Canada and freedom. Over and over in daily family prayers, he repeated his favorite quotation: "Remember them that are in bonds, as bound with them" (*Hebrews* 13:3). For years he dreamed of starting a school for black children in Randolph. Education, he thought, would be the spark that finally set off the terrible time bomb of bondage in the Southern states. Brown even got the cooperation of his family in a plan to adopt a black boy to raise with his own sons. If he had to, he said, he would suffer financial hardship and

24

buy a slave child for hard cash. As it happened, these plans came to nothing. Brown's good intentions for the future were crowded out by pressing problems of the present.

After five years in Pennsylvania, John Brown seemed to be on the sure road to success. He was known as the "Number One Man" in Randolph. Then he began to stumble—badly. During much of 1831 and 1832, he was laid low by ague, an illness much like malaria, which brought chills, high fevers, and general weakness. In March 1831 their four-year-old son sickened and died. Dianthe Brown's grief was deepened when she, too, caught the fever, then developed heart trouble. In this condition, she discovered that she was pregnant—for the seventh time in 11 years of marriage.

Would Dianthe live to bear the child? For a while it was touch and go. In August 1832, Dianthe did give birth—but the baby died almost at once. Then, three days later, Dianthe, like her newborn son, was buried in a hastily dug grave next to the Brown tannery.

John Brown was a man shattered in body and mind. He barely had strength to bury his baby boy and then his wife. His business suffered, and he went into debt. He struggled to maintain a home for his five confused children. After a few months he solved the housekeeping problem as he had back in Hudson. He hired a young woman to handle the dawn-to-dusk drudgery that was "woman's work" in those days.

In the community, eyebrows went up. Tongues started to wag. Would the new housekeeper become the next Mrs. Brown? This might have happened, but for one thing. When the workload grew too heavy, the housekeeper brought in her 16-year-old sister to do the spinning. It was the younger sister who caught John Brown's eye. Mary Anne Day was tall, strong, and sturdy. She had pitch-black hair, an ample figure, and almost no education at all. She considered John Brown her superior in almost every way. When he suddenly proposed—by a rather formal letter that he handed her after supper one evening—she was surprised and humbled to be so honored.

Mary Day and John Brown were married on July 11, 1833. She was just 17, he almost twice her age. Like Dianthe, Mary had simple and total faith in both John Brown and God. But unlike

Dianthe, Mary seemed born to bear any burden life chose to give her. (One of Mary's daughters later said that her amazing "staying qualities" probably first attracted John Brown.) Over the years Mary would know great hardship, move every few years, keep house for an often absent, crusading husband, and give birth to 13 children. Seven of these would lose their lives in childhood. Two others would be killed when young adults. In selfless sacrifice Mary Brown was a great woman, at least her husband's equal.

John Brown had regained his strength, and his tannery in Randolph was soon doing a brisk business once again. But John Brown's fortunes never bounced back from the blows suffered from 1831 to 1833. He was constantly in debt. Meanwhile, he learned from friends and relatives that Hudson, Ohio, was enjoying boom times. Randolph, Pennsylvania, remained a quiet backwater. In 1835, a rich man named Zenas Kent offered to back Brown in a new and larger tannery near Hudson.

John Brown couldn't resist the offer. Burdened by family tragedy and debt, he and his family moved to Franklin Mills, Ohio, in 1835. He still saw himself as a man who could turn failure into success—as God demanded and with God's help.

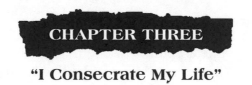

# CHAPTER THREE

## "I Consecrate My Life"

In 1836 an African American man was brutally burned to death by an angry white mob in St. Louis, Missouri. Yet the event was hardly page-one news in papers across the nation. Such things had happened many times before in states like Missouri, which allowed slavery. Undoubtedly they would happen again. Like it or not, most white people thought, this was what happened to black people who didn't "know their place."

In this case, however, the event led directly to a white mob's murder of a white man named Elijah P. Lovejoy. That killing did become HEADLINE NEWS. Abraham Lincoln called it "the most important single event that ever happened in the new world."

Elijah P. Lovejoy, a forceful writer and speaker, was then in his mid-30s. Born and educated in Maine, he had drifted west to St. Louis, Missouri, on the west bank of the Mississippi River. Trained as a minister, he had turned to newspaper work. In St. Louis he had dared to set up an abolitionist newspaper in a slave state. (People who wanted to abolish slavery, that is, to end it, were called abolitionists.)

When Lovejoy protested the brutal burning of the black man, a mob broke into his newspaper office and smashed everything in sight. His home suffered the same treatment. His young wife, shocked and paralyzed by fear, took to her bed, her year-old son beside her.

Largely because of concern for his wife, Lovejoy moved his operation across the Mississippi to the town of Alton in Illinois, a state that did not allow slavery. In a free state, he hoped, the constitutional guarantee of freedom of the press would mean something. But Alton, he discovered, was nearly as proslavery as Missouri. It was a rough waterfront town. Its dockworkers, deckhands, shopkeepers, bartenders, and gamblers all depended on a profitable steamboat trade with slave states to the south. They wanted no trouble from an abolitionist with what they considered a "funny" Maine accent.

Lovejoy's printing press was smashed as soon as he arrived. He refused to give up. He ordered another press and started to publish the Alton *Observer*. When the second press was thrown into the Mississippi, he ordered a third. Nothing, it seemed, would stop Elijah P. Lovejoy. Not a mob who seized him, with the tar and feathers all prepared. Not threats against his wife, who now seldom left her bed. Not even a boozy crowd of waterfront scum who attacked his house with rocks and drove his wife and son to the attic in numb terror.

Tension rose to a flash point as the third press was also smashed. Then a group of leading citizens decided that something had to be done. They prepared what they termed a compromise and called a community meeting. But the so-called compromise offered Lovejoy nothing but useless praise for his ideals and courage. For the safety of himself and his family, he was told, he must give up his newspaper and move out of town. If he refused, it would be his own decision. He would have to suffer the consequences.

As the meeting neared its end, Lovejoy himself rose to speak. He began in a low, serious voice that rose with conviction until it brought tears to all listeners—and finally to the speaker himself. He had a *right* to publish his views on slavery, he said. That right was given to him by both God and the Constitution of the United States of America. Now nothing could stop him. Nothing—no one—could disgrace him. "I, and I alone, can disgrace myself." The deepest disgrace, he said, would be for he himself to ignore the will of God. As Jesus Christ had died for him, so now, if he had to, he would die for Jesus Christ.

"No sir," Lovejoy ended his moving speech, "the contest has commenced here; and here it must be finished. Before God, and you all, I here pledge myself to continue it, if need be, till death. If I fail, my grave shall be made in Alton."

Four days later Elijah P. Lovejoy was shot to death as he tried to defend his fourth press from mob attack. News of the event quickly spread throughout the North. Abolitionists called meetings in Boston, New York, Philadelphia, and other cities. These

In 1837, a mob in Alton, Illinois, destroyed the office and press of Elijah P. Lovejoy's antislavery newspaper and killed Lovejoy.

large meetings were echoed by smaller gatherings in places like Hudson, Ohio.

The Hudson meeting was held in the Congregational Church near the end of November 1837. Speaker after speaker rose to give tribute to Lovejoy. Owen Brown, in spite of the stammer in his voice and the tears in his eyes, reported on Lovejoy's last speech. Most abolitionists in Hudson had always hoped that slavery could be ended in a peaceful way—by shaming the slave owners into love of other humans. But now, what did Lovejoy's death mean? Would it be right to take up arms—not to free the millions of enslaved people but to defend the rights of another Elijah P. Lovejoy? The proslavery people clearly would stop at nothing. Should force be met with force? "The question now," one speaker said, "is no longer alone, 'Can the slaves be made free?' but 'Are we free or are we slaves under Southern mob law?'"

In the back of the church, one man in his late 30s did not

stand up to speak until the very end of the meeting. When he did so, his face was so serious, his manner so commanding, that all turned to listen. With his right hand raised, palm out, he uttered only a single, slow sentence:

"Here before God, in the presence of these witnesses, I consecrate my life to the destruction of slavery."

That man was John Brown.

What had happened in the United States? Particularly since John Brown's birth, what had happened to bring the mob to Elijah P. Lovejoy's office and the abolitionists to the Hudson church?

Slavery had long been part of the American scene. The first black Africans were forcibly brought as indentured servants to Jamestown, Virginia, at about the same time as the Pilgrims arrived in New England. Since that time, there had been enslaved people in each of the 13 original colonies. When John Brown was born, in 1800, there were almost a million enslaved black Africans, North and South. The U.S. Constitution, without ever using the word *slavery*, had recognized slavery as a feature of American life.

The Northern states, however, had begun passing laws against slavery, even before the U.S. Constitution had been ratified in 1788. These laws usually did not free all of the enslaved people all at once. Most Northern laws freed only slave children born after a certain date, and then only when they became 21 (or 25 or 28). The laws were well meaning, but the results were sometimes bad. Whole families lost almost all hope for freedom when they were sold off to the South, where no such laws existed. A few of the enslaved people kept in the North were still there in bondage on the eve of the Civil War.

At the time of John Brown's birth, there was still some hope that slavery might come to a gradual end in the South as well. In 1800, Thomas Jefferson had been elected as the third President of the United States. Jefferson was a Southern slaveholder. Yet he was also a man who considered slavery an evil in the eyes of God. How was this possible?

Jefferson dreamed of a nation where "all Men are created equal," entitled to "Life, Liberty, and the Pursuit of Happiness"—

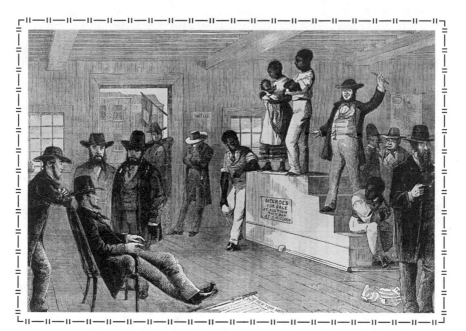

During John Brown's lifetime, auctions of enslaved people similar to the ones in this 1861 engraving were common in the South.

as he had written in the 1776 Declaration of Independence. But in a practical sense, he saw no way to free the slaves. Enslaved people were considered property and were accepted as such by the Constitution. It was useless to think of *paying* all the slave owners for this expensive and valuable property. The cost would be staggering. Where would the money come from? Also, what would happen to nearly a million people suddenly granted their freedom? To keep the slaves "in their place," laws were passed making it illegal to teach them to read or write. Most lacked the skills needed to earn a living. What would they do? Drifting armies of freed people—helpless, landless, unemployed, and hungry—might become real armies. Who would blame them for taking up arms and treating their former masters as they themselves had been treated? "We have the wolf by the ears," Jefferson wrote, "and we can neither hold him, nor safely let him go. Justice is in one scale, and self preservation in the other."

In 1800, the year John Brown was born and Thomas Jefferson

31

elected President, the great Gabriel Slave Rebellion occurred in Virginia. "General" Gabriel Prosser, a fearless and intelligent 24-year-old slave, organized a secret liberation army of a thousand men. His plan was to conquer Richmond, the state capital of Virginia. But as luck would have it, a fierce storm blew up just as the march began. The area between Gabriel Prosser's army and Richmond turned into an impassable swamp. Roads were washed away. Bridges collapsed. The army of a thousand dissolved along with everything else. As usual in slave rebellions, the leaders were caught and led to the noose.

Three things can be said about the revolts of enslaved Blacks in the South. First, they were heroic. Their daring leaders hold a high place in history. Second, they never succeeded. White power was just too strong. Third, they made life worse for the great mass of enslaved people. Slave uprisings brought new laws to keep black people down. Certain books were banned—and most slaves could not read them anyway. Arms were strictly controlled. Slave gatherings of any size brought savage beatings and sometimes death. Even church services were often banned, for where better for Blacks to plot bloody revenge on their masters?

Jefferson's great hope was that slavery not be allowed to expand. But that remained only a dream. The invention of the cotton gin in 1793 had made cotton fiber preparation easier. The rise of the cotton textile mills in the North and in Britain also encouraged the boom in cotton plantations in the South. As John Brown grew up, the slave empire of the South pushed forward with brushfire speed. Louisiana, Mississippi, and Alabama joined the Union as slave states. The Missouri Compromise of 1820 secured slavery's future south of the 36°30´ line extending westward from Missouri's southern border. The compromise passed by Congress divided the huge Louisiana Purchase at that line. North of the line, except for the new state of Missouri, slavery was not allowed. South of the line, slavery could legally spread. To keep the total number of free states and slave states equal, Maine was admitted as a free state and Missouri as a slave state.

By 1830, the slave population had passed 2 million. Slave owners claimed that cheap slave labor was absolutely necessary for the growing of cotton, a crop that made many a Southern plantation owner rich in a few short years. The production of Southern cotton increased fourfold from 1810 to 1830. It would double, double again, and then nearly once again before the beginning of the Civil War.

The expansion of slavery greatly disturbed some people in the North—not many, but a few. About 1830, these few began to make their voices heard. In 1831, a Bostonian named William Lloyd Garrison started an abolitionist paper, *The Liberator*. John Brown could now read pamphlets describing slavery at its worst—the near starvation; the lashing of laggards in the cotton fields; men stripped naked, hung up by the hands and beaten into senselessness. Flesh branded with hot irons. Fingers and ears cut off. His head full of such horrors, John Brown could only cheer when he read, also in 1831, of the Nat Turner Slave Rebellion in Virginia. Turner's band of 70 Blacks managed to kill 57 Whites before they were stopped. Of course, Turner was hanged, as were many other Blacks, some of them innocent.

Considering the westward growth of the slave empire, it might be supposed that the Northern abolitionists of the 1830s would find an eager audience. Sadly, such was not the case. When the first abolitionists stood up to speak, they were often pelted with garbage—or with stones. Garrison himself was once nearly killed by a lynch mob.

Most Northern states had what were called black laws. In John Brown's Ohio, for instance, a black man had to prove he was

William Lloyd Garrison established his abolitionist newspaper, *The Liberator*, in Boston. He condemned slavery as a national sin.

Nat Turner being captured six weeks after leading a revolt of
enslaved people in Virginia in 1831. He was tried and hanged.

legally free in order to get a job. His promise to keep out of trouble had to be guaranteed by two white citizens of known character. His children could not attend public schools. He could forget about voting, although not about his taxes. If he or his wife had to travel, the trip would probably be made on top of the stagecoach, rather than inside. Free Blacks usually could not eat or sleep in accommodations that served white people. In the workplace, Whites often refused to labor beside Blacks, who were left only those jobs no one else would take. Most Northern Blacks lived in shanties. Many Whites considered Blacks to be little more than human beasts of burden.

Things were slightly better in New England—but only slightly. In 1833, a young Quaker woman in Connecticut was peacefully trying to run a school for black girls. Prudence Crandall's neighbors objected—violently. They attacked her school with pickaxes

White bigots forced Prudence Crandall's academy for black girls
in Canterbury, Connecticut, to close in 1834.

and iron bars. They put poison in her well. They tried to burn the
school to the ground. When these steps failed, the citizens of
Canterbury appealed to the Connecticut legislature. The law-
makers then made it illegal to teach black children from out of
state. (Most of Prudence Crandall's 15 students were not
Connecticut natives.) Crandall was thrown into jail, and her students declared vagrants, that is, people who have no established
home and who wander idly from place to place with no legal
means of support. The authorities then dusted off an old
vagrancy law. A warrant was issued for the arrest of a 17-year-old
girl, whose legal punishment was to feel the whip "on the naked
body not exceeding ten stripes."

Meanwhile, 400 miles away, a tanner named John Brown fur-
rowed his brow as he tried to determine what it all meant. Slavery
seemed to damage the soul of all people in the nation, North and
South, White and Black. Brown wondered what meaning he
could now find in the Declaration of Independence and the
Golden Rule. Part of that meaning, he finally decided, he would
have to find in action. Words meant nothing until they were
backed by deeds: "I consecrate my life . . ."

35

# CHAPTER FOUR

## Businessman Brown

In 1837 John Brown pledged his life to the battle against slavery. But at first he could take no action. After all, he had no regular job. He had a family of 10 to feed. And he was up to his ears in trouble.

Brown had moved back to Ohio to be the "know-how" half of a tanning partnership with Zenas Kent. The wealthy Kent was to provide the money. But John Brown was not made to be a partner with anyone on an equal basis. He had to be in charge. In this case, his partnership with Kent ended even before the tannery building was finished. Brown was then stuck in Franklin Mills (now Kent), Ohio, without an income. He found work for a time using his team of oxen to help dig a new canal that would run east from Akron, Ohio, into Pennsylvania.

John Brown was down on his luck, but the rest of northeastern Ohio seemed to be booming. The good times had started with the completion of the Erie Canal across New York State. Ohio farmers could now send their foodstuffs via the canal to the Hudson River and then downriver to New York City and other population centers in the East. The Ohio farmers' good fortune meant rising land prices. Then the first small factories came to Ohio. The success of the Erie Canal started a rush of canal building. The Ohio Canal ran from Lake Erie south through Akron. John Brown himself worked on the Pennsylvania–Ohio Canal, intended to feed into the Ohio Canal, which was connected to points east.

In Ohio, good land near both waterpower and canal transportation rose and rose in value. On these sites, certainly, would be the great factories of the future. Franklin Mills, Ohio, seemed perfectly located. Just to the northwest was the Cuyahoga River, with waterfalls to provide swiftly flowing water to turn the waterwheels for mills and factories. To the south ran the new canal.

Farmland that once sold for $20 an acre now went for hundreds. A new Franklin Land Company had pieced together a huge tract, or area of land, for development. Rich investors in the East were said to have great plans for the Franklin area. It was to become the silk capital of the nation. Silkworms were already on their way from Asia, to start spinning a huge new industry.

Land fever was in the air that John Brown breathed every day. People could buy land, hold it briefly, and then resell it at a much higher price. Huge profits were being made. Before long the spirit of speculation infected him, too. A man named Frederick Haymaker owned a 95-acre farm near the Franklin Land Company property. Brown learned that Haymaker would sell for about $7,000. (This was a huge amount of money, for at that time a worker on one of the new canals earned from 75¢ to $2 a day, depending on the skill of the worker.) Brown borrowed enough money for the down payment from Seth Thompson, his old business partner, and others. With borrowed money, Brown then "owned" the Haymaker farm. Soon he was busy surveying and

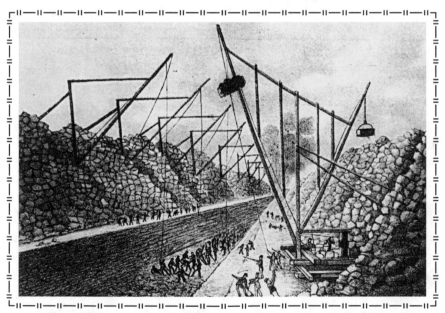

New York's successful Erie Canal set off an Ohio canal-building and land-selling boom in which John Brown participated.

naming avenues and streets. Factory sites and housing lots were staked out and priced. For instance, a large three-quarter-acre lot at the corner of Franklin Street and Haymaker would be $900. A smaller lot for a more modest house could be purchased for a mere $100. He expected to get rich.

When the first buyers showed up, Brown was overjoyed—even though they brought promises to pay rather than cold cash. This little success launched him into a feverish spiral of land buying. Before long he "owned" a house and farm near Hudson (six miles from Franklin Mills). Then he bought two other farms, one of them a magnificent showplace, a paradise called Westlands.

The full story of Brown's wheeling and dealing would take a book this size to explain. To this day, his business practices are open to question. Over the years, even Brown's supporters have had to admit that his sunny hopes forced him into shady dealing at times. His critics state flatly that he was a thoroughly dishonest scoundrel.

Basically, what John Brown did was this. He would borrow money from banks or individuals—often from more than one source—to make at least the down payment on a property. Then, as the "owner" of that property, he would borrow even more money, pledging the property as a guarantee of the loan. This new money would be used to purchase still another property. In theory, the process could go on forever—all without John Brown putting up any real money of his own. Money was easy to borrow at the time. Personal notes, or promises to pay, often circulated just like money. Some companies also issued notes that people accepted and commonly used as cash. Ohio state banks were allowed to issue "real" paper money—often backed by nothing more than promises to pay from people like John Brown.

Brown's dream of easy riches began to spin out of control in the very year it began—1836. In July of that year, President Andrew Jackson issued an executive order called the Specie Circular. From then on, only specie (gold or silver money) could be used to buy public lands from the government. The goal was to curb land speculation and to stop the enormous growth of paper money. Notes from state banks began to lose value as everyone scrambled for specie. The days of easy money were over. Land values collapsed. This brought on the Panic of 1837 and a six-year national economic depression in which many banks and companies went out of business and thousands of people lost their savings and their jobs.

As the value of land collapsed, so did John Brown's hopes. Work on the Pennsylvania–Ohio Canal was stopped. Water from the Cuyahoga River was diverted away from Franklin toward factories in Akron. Silkworms from Asia proved not to like the cold Ohio weather. Almost overnight, John Brown was left with a bundle of 1836 debts he could not pay off at the low 1837 land prices. He was trapped. One by one, people to whom John Brown owed money brought their cases to court. He was sued more than 20 times.

This 1837 cartoon depicts jobless workers, a begging widow and orphan, and a crowd rushing to withdraw money from a bank.

Desperately, John Brown did everything he could think of to scrape up a few dollars. He did some surveying and odd jobs. He tried breeding racehorses for a track at Warren, Ohio. In 1838 and 1839, he drove huge herds of cattle east to sell in Connecticut. On the return trip in 1838, he brought some purebred Saxony sheep, with which he hoped to start a thriving business. On the return trip in 1839, he brought nothing but bad news.

In Connecticut, Brown had really impressed Tertius Wadsworth and Joseph Wells, cattle dealers in West Hartford. In 1839, Brown somehow managed to get his hands on $5,500 of the firm's money. The details, today, are cloudy. Brown may have stolen it. Or he may have been given the money for future cattle purchases. At any rate, Brown seems to have immediately sent the $5,500 back to Ohio to save his beloved Westlands farm. Wadsworth & Wells grew suspicious and threatened legal action. To avoid arrest, Brown gave Wadsworth & Wells $2,800 that he had just received from another company to buy wool. When the wool company demanded an explanation, Brown had none. He had no choice but to confess and beg for mercy.

Brown hurried back to Ohio, only to face the lawsuits waiting for him there. He opened up his old tanning business near Hudson. Unable to get any money out of a strapped John Brown, the people with claims against him kept going to court, demanding that he sell one possession, then another, to pay his debts. In June 1840, Brown's personal property was auctioned off. He lost his furniture, his farm equipment, even his prize Saxony sheep. Then in October, the court ordered that Westlands go on the auction block to satisfy still more claims. Brown was disgusted when his favorite farm sold for only $1,681. This was less than a third what he had paid for it in 1836.

At this point John Brown put himself above the law. He refused to recognize the sale. He insisted that he still owned Westlands. In truth, the Westlands case was a complicated matter, since there was more than one claim to the land. In his typical double-dealing fashion, Brown had borrowed twice with the same property as guarantee. Since he had paid one loan back, he thought he still owned the land. But on the other hand, the farm had been sold to satisfy claims against Brown that had nothing to do with the Westlands property. The court was undoubtedly right in its action, but Brown could see things only his way.

John Brown wrapped himself in bitter pride and vowed that the new owner would not set foot on Westlands soil. With his oldest sons and a few older muskets, Brown holed up in an ancient log house on the property. There he would wait night and day, he said, until the new owner gave up. When Amos Chamberlain, the buyer, arrived, he saw that Brown meant business. So did a local constable with a small posse. The Browns' guns were loaded. The smell of trouble was in the air. The constable then sent for the county sheriff, who managed to outfox Brown without a showdown. The sheriff waited until Brown finally left the log house to look in at his tannery. There Brown was quietly surprised and arrested. His sons, hearing of their father's arrest, gave up, too. Soon three men named Brown were behind bars in the Akron jail.

They did not stay there long. John Brown promised to appear in court if called, and the sheriff unlocked the cell door. Undoubtedly, Brown had worked his old personal magic on this sheriff. It was the same spellbinding manner that had won Brown trust and money so many times before. How could one distrust a man who looked and acted like John Brown? His honest blue-gray eyes met yours. He was so direct, so earnest, so sincere. He could not help quoting the Bible at times. As he talked, he bent his thin shoulders forward slightly. He had a habit of holding his hands out before him as he spoke, fingers spread and palms down, raising and lowering the hands to punctuate his points. This was a man who liked to boast that he could make a dog leave the room simply by looking at it.

John Brown's personal history during these years of trouble is fairly well known. There are official records, Brown's letters to others, and the accounts of several people. But what of his wife, Mary? We can only imagine what Mary's life must have been like. Between 1835 and 1840 she gave birth to five boys: Watson, Salmon, Charles, Oliver, and Peter. During this period she had to move at least six times. Her husband was sometimes away for weeks and even months at a time. Money was almost always a problem, at times so scarce that buying postage stamps was difficult. ("Oh, we were poor!" Jason Brown wrote later.) Mary Brown

**41**

also endured periods of illness, although she was by nature a strong, vigorous woman. Yet throughout her trials, she seems to have remained absolutely loyal to her husband. His letters to her show that the couple shared a tender concern and real love.

There is also the question of John Brown's antislavery activity during this period. Clearly, driven by dreams of riches and then by threats of jail, he had little time for other people. It can be said, however, that part of the reason for his pursuit of wealth was to have money in hand for what he began to call his "greatest or principal object." By this he clearly meant freeing the slaves. Brown had no love of money in and for itself. He had simple tastes and loved plainness in all things. He actually worried that money would lead him into temptations frowned upon by God. "I hope that entire leanness of soul may not attend any little success in business," he wrote his son John Jr.

Also, John Brown did what he could for African Americans as chances came along. In the Hudson church in 1837, he had publicly declared that he was consecrating his life to the destruction of slavery. About that time, too, he took care to change the seating arrangements in church. Brown could never understand why black people always sat in the back near the stove. More than once he suddenly rose in the Brown family pew, interrupting the preacher. Then he led his own family to the back of the church, where he signaled to the African Americans. As the large crowd looked on in puzzled silence, he led the Blacks forward and seated them in the now-vacant Brown family pew. The Browns then sat in the back. This practice won him few friends; he was considered a troublemaker. A home visit by church leaders only turned Brown's stubbornness into stone. Throughout his life Brown remained only a now-and-then churchgoer. He seldom agreed with the minister, especially on the God-given rights of black people.

After the forced sale of Brown's property in 1840, his fortunes began to brighten somewhat. In 1841, a wealthy man named Herman Oviatt offered Brown a partnership in a sheep-raising venture in Richfield, Ohio. As usual, Brown was to provide the "know-how" and work, the other partner the money. Brown had given Oviatt a rather dirty double deal on some of his property

John Brown failed at many businesses, including selling land,
breeding racehorses, selling cattle, and exporting wool to England.

43

schemes, but now Oviatt expressed his continued faith in Brown as a basically good man. Since Brown still owed Oviatt over $5,000, however, Oviatt may simply have wanted to keep Brown under his thumb. At any rate, Oviatt had nothing but admiration for Brown's skill with sheep.

John Brown's own high opinion of himself as a "practical *Shepherd*" was shared by everyone. Already he was traveling around to meetings of sheep raisers. There he gave talks on such topics as the treatment of sheep diseases and the cleaning and grading of wool. Although to most people—then as now—one sheep looks pretty much like another, to John Brown they were as individual as human beings. He claimed that he could recognize each sheep in a flock of hundreds. If another sheep joined his flock, he said, he could spot it at once. He liked nothing more than rescuing lambs that sometimes looked dead on the ground on a frosty morning. First, he would gather up the lamb in his arms and carry it into the house. There he would heat water in the family washtub. As the surrounding water warmed its body, the lamb would start to show signs of life. Then, Brown would hold the lamb on his lap, drying the fleece and rubbing it hard. Finally, he would take the scampering white lamb back to the flock for its mother's milk. Brown noted that even in a noisy flock of hundreds, every lamb could recognize its own mother's bleating. That proved sheep were individuals, didn't it?

Although Brown's sheep raising went well, it did little to ease his many debts. In 1842, he applied for legal bankruptcy under a new federal law. (In a bankruptcy, a court distributes what a person owns among others to whom money is owed, then declares that person legally free of all past debts.) The court's list of possessions the Brown family was allowed to keep still exists. It is sad in its pathetic detail: "10 dining Plates," it starts, "1 Set of Cups and Saucers . . . 1 Cider Barrel . . . 1 Bushel Dryed Apples . . . 20 Galls Soap . . . 11 Bibles & Testaments . . . 2 Hogs . . . 19 Hens . . . 2 Saddles . . . 10 Women's and Girl's Dresses. . . ."

A much harsher blow fell the very next year. In September 1843, an epidemic of dysentery swept through the Richfield community. Dysentery is a sometimes deadly disease whose main symptom is severe diarrhea. The Browns were not spared. John

Brown sat up night after night nursing sick children so that Mary could rest. But by the end of September, four of their children were dead. As he had done before, John Brown hammered together simple caskets and buried their children nearby. He praised God for whatever divine plan had given his children early entry into Paradise. He thanked God for those family members left with him to share this short season of trial on earth. Besides his wife, Mary, these were the children from his first marriage: John Jr., now 22 and out of the house; gentle Jason, 20; Owen, 18, who couldn't use one arm; lively Ruth, 14; unpredictable, flighty Frederick, 12; and the remaining children from his marriage with Mary: Watson 7; Salmon 6; and Oliver, 4.

The following year, 1844, John Brown ended his partnership with Oviatt. Right away he entered a similar sheep-raising arrangement with Simon Perkins of Akron, Ohio. Perkins was an enormously wealthy man who lived on family money. Thus, he had no burning desire to see Brown show a profit at once. Perkins was ideal partner in another way, too. A short, rather mild man, he was quite willing to let his new partner make all the decisions. "I had no controversy with John Brown," Perkins said later, "for it would have done no good." Perkins was even willing to let Brown spend some of his time on the road, speaking at meetings and dealing in sheep. The older Brown children could easily care for the flock in Akron, which soon became known as one of the best in the United States.

As John Brown traveled in Ohio, northern Virginia, and western Pennsylvania and New York, his interest turned from sheep farming to the wool business itself. Most of the woolen mills—the buyers of the sheep's fleece—were in New England. These mills sent out agents to buy wool from individual farmers. Brown became sure that the agents buying the fleece were, in effect, fleecing the farmers. The isolated farmer had to accept the agent's opinion on the grade of his wool. The farmer usually had to accept the agent's price as well. To John Brown, this was more than just a matter of business. It was a great *wrong*, and it had to be righted.

In 1846, Brown proposed that the firm of Perkins & Brown expand its operations. He would open an office in Springfield,

A Massachusetts woolen mill in the 1840s. Brown was unsuccessful at buying, grading, and selling wool to such mills.

Massachusetts. There he would buy wool sent by farmers, grade it accurately, and get the best price from the mill owners. For these services, Perkins & Brown would take two cents a pound for all wool they handled. Brown was sure most of the sheep farmers he knew would sign up. And if most sheep farmers cooperated, Brown thought, he could soon control both the supply and the price of wool.

Simon Perkins agreed to the plan, although with some doubts. He knew Brown was a bankrupt who had failed again and again. But Brown seemed so *sure* that the business would succeed! Brown met all Perkins's objections as soon as he voiced them. Jason and Owen would stay in Akron and give the flock excellent care. John Jr. would go with his father. As soon as he could, Brown would send for Mary and the smaller children to

46

join him at a new home in Massachusetts. Brown's Springfield operation was a disaster from the very beginning. Observers at the time realized that he was an honest and honorable man. He was willing to work sunup to sundown, grading and bagging the 60 or so bales of fleece that came to his warehouse every day. But men who had traded in wool for years shook their heads. One rival wool merchant, a man named Aaron Erickson, said Brown had an "almost childlike ignorance" of the fine points of the business. According to Erickson, John Brown put himself above "the plainest and simplest laws of commerce" and "would hear no opposing argument."

Perhaps John Brown had too much business at first. Even with his son's help, he could not keep up with acknowledgments or accounts. But the basic flaw, according to another observer, was that by nature Brown "was no *trader.*" He thought that his own opinions overruled the law of supply and demand. He priced his lower-grade fleece too low. Brown had little patience with farmers who sent him wool full of dried mud, manure, straw, and so forth; fleece from his own flock was always spotless. He priced the best wool too high. As a result, the New England woolen mills snapped up Brown's inferior fleece and left him stuck with many bales of the better product he so much admired. He told people he was holding his high-quality wool back until prices improved. He accused the mill owners of meeting in secret to set prices unfairly. It was war between the woolen mills and John Brown, and Brown was never a man to back down.

Meanwhile, the sheep farmers began to demand payment for the fine wool that now swelled Brown's Springfield warehouse. Some of them sued. Others sued because Brown had sold their lower-grade fleece below the market price. A woolen mill sued as well, claiming that Brown had shipped fleece of a lower quality than paid for. Brown was forced to take the step that had led him to destruction before—borrowing money from banks. Yet he kept hoping that next week . . . next month . . . next year . . . the days of golden fleece would come at last.

By the spring of 1849, Perkins & Brown was deeply in debt. Brown was a desperate man once again. Then, for some reason no one has ever been able to figure out, he became convinced that he could sell his fleece in England at a high price. Thomas Musgrave, an Englishman who ran a Massachusetts woolen mill, told Brown that his wool would bring less, not more, in England. Aaron Erickson paid Brown another call. Didn't Brown know that the British market was flooded with fleece? That prices were headed down, not up? But, once again, Brown "would hear no opposing argument." Erickson threw up his hands and walked out. He wondered if Brown was off his head.

Sadly for John Brown, the predictions of Musgrave and Erickson came true. Brown and 200,000 pounds of fleece crossed the Atlantic by steamship. After weeks of pointless bargaining, Brown was forced to sell his wool for what little he could get.

For most purposes, John Brown's wool business in Springfield came to an end in 1849. The lawsuits, however, continued. Brown formally closed the office in 1851, but the legal battles went on and on. Since Brown had no money to pay the court awards, the funds had to come from the deep pockets of his partner, Simon Perkins. In the end Perkins lost about $60,000—the better part of a million dollars in today's money.

## CHAPTER FIVE

## The Grand Plan Revealed

There are several reasons for John Brown's failure as a wool merchant. He had a poor head for paperwork. He regarded his own opinions as facts beyond dispute. He refused to listen to others. And perhaps equally important, his main interest at the time lay elsewhere. Even as he graded wool in his Springfield warehouse, his "greatest or principal object" in life was to free America's 4 million enslaved people.

In his business travels, Brown made a point of seeking out persons who shared this object. For the most part, he avoided white abolitionists. In Brown's view, these people did nothing but talk, talk, talk. What had more than 200 years of endless talk done? Absolutely nothing. Slavery had continued to spread like a vile and bitter weed. During Brown's years in Springfield, the Mexican War (1846–48) added the whole Southwest to the nation. Would the slave empire of the South now push across the continent to the Pacific Ocean? To John Brown, it looked like that. And all the talk in the world would do nothing to stop it.

No, John Brown liked men of action. He preferred meeting with men like the Reverends J. W. Logan and Henry Highland Garnet. Logan and Garnet were African American leaders in upstate New York. Both had escaped from slavery. Both preached violent rebellion. "Rather die freemen than live to be slaves," Garnet had told a meeting of the National Negro Convention as early as 1843. "Remember that you are FOUR MILLIONS!"

Among the black leaders who emerged in the 1840s, none became better known than Frederick Douglass. An escaped slave turned abolitionist, Douglass seemed born to play his unique and heroic role in history. His tall, commanding figure and noble profile rivaled George Washington's. As a mental giant he rivaled Thomas Jefferson. As a speaker he probably had no rival. His voice was a mighty organ than could move people to tears.

Douglass in person was living proof of everything he said. People found it hard to believe that this outstanding human being had actually been born in bondage. Yet this man had spent his first 21 years in slavery. He had been there. He knew.

John Brown heard of Frederick Douglass in the early 1840s and wanted to meet him. But Douglass was a busy man. The historic meeting did not take place until 1847. By that time, Douglass at the age of only 30 was a famous writer and speaker. Brown, by contrast, was 47, and few people outside the wool trade had ever heard of him.

In later years, Frederick Douglass wrote a detailed account of his first meeting with John Brown. Douglass had arrived in Springfield, Massachusetts, and sought out the firm of Perkins &

After lecturing in Great Britain in 1847, the famous abolitionist Frederick Douglass met with John Brown in Massachusetts.

Brown. He found Brown at work in a brick building downtown. It seemed to be "a flourishing business." "In person," Douglass recalled, Brown was "lean and sinewy, of the best new England mould, built for times of trouble." Brown stood "straight and symmetrical as a mountain pine." The two men soon left the wool warehouse for Brown's home.

Walking "with a long springing, race-horse step," Brown led his guest to a small wooden house on a side street. In contrast to the "flourishing business," the house was barely respectable. "Plain as was the outside," Douglass wrote, "the inside was plainer . . . no sofas, no cushions, no curtains, no carpets, no easy rocking chairs. . . ." Mary Brown and the children greeted Douglass with smiling faces. A supper of potatoes, cabbage, and beef soup was served on a pine table "innocent of paint, veneering, varnish or tablecloth." There were, of course, no servants— which Douglass thought just fine. "No hired help passed from kitchen to dining room, staring in amazement at the colored man at the white man's table."

Douglass soon noted that Brown was clearly the master in his own home. Douglass wrote that Brown's "wife believed in him, and his children observed him with reverence. . . . Certainly I never felt myself in the presence of a stronger religious influence than while in this house." Talk of "God and duty" ran through everything Brown said, "and his family supplied a ready 'Amen.'"

The boys, Salmon and Watson, helped Mary Brown clear the table and start on the dishes. Then John Brown got down to the business at hand. He had a secret plan, he told Douglass, that would free the slaves in the South. For years he had been waiting for the appearance of black leaders in the North who might help him. Now such leaders had arrived. Brown would share this secret plan with Frederick Douglass and appeal for his help.

Then John Brown brought out a map of the eastern United States. He spread it out on the bare pine table. He pointed to the long north-south range of the Appalachian Mountains. This chain of mountains stretches from the Canadian border down through Pennsylvania and into the Southern states as far as Georgia. "These mountains," Brown said, "are the basis of my plan. God has given the strength of these hills to freedom; they were placed here to aid the emancipation [freedom] of your race; they are full of natural forts, where one man for defense would be equal to a hundred for attack. . . ."

The words then tumbled out of John Brown's mouth. A small force of 25 men, he said, could set up the first outpost in the mountains of Virginia. From that base, agents would be sent out to enlist enslaved people on both sides of the mountains. Soon the force would expand to "one hundred hardy men." In the mountains, Brown was sure, they would be safe from any attack. As this liberation army moved farther into the Southern mountains, more enslaved people would swell the ranks. The movement "would run off slaves in large numbers, retain the strong and brave ones in the mountains, and send the weak and timid ones to the North by the underground Rail-road." (The Underground Railroad was the system of cooperation among active antislavery people in which escaping enslaved people in the South were secretly helped to reach the North or Canada.) Brown then reminded Douglass of the great Nat Turner Slave Rebellion in Virginia 16 years earlier. Turner would have succeeded, Brown claimed, if only he had been near a mountain stronghold where 100 armed men stood ready to help him. What did Frederick Douglass think of this plan?

"From 8 o'clock in the evening till 3 in the morning," Douglass remembered, "Brown and I sat face to face, he arguing in favor of his plan, and I finding all the objections I could against it." Douglass worried that Brown's scheme might lead to a general slave uprising in the South. Both men knew that such a rebellion would quickly become a bloodbath for Blacks. No, Brown argued, such a slaughter was exactly what he was trying to prevent. He again stressed that his was a *mountain* plan. The slaves would not try to turn on their masters and take over the plantations. Brown believed that the Appalachian Mountains had been put there by God, like a long finger pointing deep into the South, for one very special divine purpose. Brown would set up a temporary government in these mountains. His men there would never fire except in self-defense. There would be no bloodbath of either White or Black on the plantations.

How would the men in the mountains be fed and supplied?

This was not an impossible problem, Brown believed. "Slavery was a state of war, [Brown] said, to which the slaves were unwilling parties and consequently they had a right to anything necessary to their peace and freedom." In other words, enslaved people who had been held as property now had a right to seize whatever property they needed to gain their freedom. Escaping people would bring along, on their shoulders, everything from sacks of ground corn and flour to the best well-cured hams hanging in their masters' smokehouses. Of course, Brown admitted, some money would be needed to get the project started.

At this point in the conversation, Brown indicated, in the shadows cast by lamplight, the drabness of the room in which they sat. He lived this way, he explained, to save money for that great and principal object.

Douglass continued to ask questions: Suppose the mountain project did succeed. What would happen then?

Brown's response was exact: "He believed this movement would weaken slavery in two ways—first by making slave property insecure, it would become undesirable; and secondly it would keep the antislavery agitation alive and public attention fixed upon it, and thus lead to the adoption of measures to abolish the evil altogether." Brown was sure that the slave empire was ready to topple; all it needed was the right kind of push.

After a short night's sleep, Frederick Douglass left the Brown household somewhat confused. Would Brown's plan really work? Douglass honestly did not know. Up to this point, Douglass had always agreed with the nonviolent plans of William Lloyd Garrison and other leading abolitionists. But now he wondered. Soon he would be saying that—well, just maybe—force might be necessary after all.

The John Brown that Frederick Douglass met in 1847 was definitely a man living a divided life. With one hand, he managed his Springfield wool business. With the other, he did all he could to help African Americans. In 1847, Brown was also planning to start a high school for Blacks in Canada, where many escaped slaves were living. The project came to nothing for the usual reason—lack of money. During the same year, Brown became interested in still another project. This was Gerrit Smith's colony of black farm families in North Elba in northern New York State.

Gerrit Smith was one of the richest men in the United States. He was also a marvelously good man. He liked nothing better than giving thousands of acres or piles of inherited wealth to various worthy causes. One of Smith's favorite causes was the betterment of African Americans in the United States. In the 1840s, he announced that he would give thousands of acres to hundreds of landless black farmers. In 1846, he started an African American community in North Elba, high in the Adirondack Mountains of New York State. Ten black families were given 40 acres each. They built crude log shanties and did their best to survive.

John Brown was delighted by Smith's New Elba experiment. But he was disappointed when he heard how things were going. Most of the black people in far-north North Elba had little experience as farmers, and none at all as homesteaders. The New Elba colony was hanging on for life in a difficult area to farm.

In the spring of 1848, John Brown left his wool business to pay a call on Gerrit Smith in Peterboro, New York. By the time Brown arrived, he was bubbling with ideas of his own. He told Smith that he would like to move to North Elba, join the black community, and develop a farm himself. His whole life had been an education he could now share with the black homesteaders. He knew how to turn forests into fields. He knew how to turn native wood into houses and barns. He knew how to raise prizewinning sheep and cattle. Most of all, Brown told Smith, he knew that he wanted to help black people. If he could move to North Elba, Brown said, he could "look after them in all ways and be a kind of father to them."

Gerrit Smith was definitely interested. Before long he would become one of Brown's most devoted admirers. Smith's money would back Brown's know-how in a new kind of venture.

In the fall of 1848, John Brown again left Springfield, this time to visit the black community at North Elba. He was shocked at what he saw. Ten decent black families had been offered the chance to take up land in this high, cold, and remote area. Then they had been left there to survive or starve. So far, they had barely survived.

But the area pleased John Brown. Timbucto, as the black

community was called, was surrounded by a ring of high mountains, It was harsh, rugged country. The clear, sparkling air; the sweeping peak-studded views; the bubbling, busy little streams; the towering cliffs of black rock as one neared North Elba—all worked their magic on John Brown. Perhaps there was something about the solid, sturdy, and enduring quality of the scenery that mirrored John Brown's soul. At any rate, he decided to leave Springfield as soon as possible. He was not by nature a city man. In North Elba he could again be on the land, helping friendly black neighbors as he lived out his life. If the chance ever came, he might even get some North Elba Blacks to join him in the Virginia mountains.

The next year was 1849, and Brown's wool business in Springfield was on a rapid downhill slide. He could not move to

Mary Brown and two of her children, Anne (left) and Sarah,
in a photo taken about the time they had settled in North Elba.

This 1850 photo of John Brown was taken soon after he had moved his family to North Elba in the Adirondack Mountains.

North Elba himself, but he did the next best thing. Before his disastrous wool-business trip to England, he moved Mary and the children to the Adirondack community. Once again, the Brown family possessions went into the rear of an ox cart. Mary, who was ill at the time, rode in the front of the cart with their two small daughters, Anne and Sarah. John Brown, of course, trudged along beside the single ox. Ruth, now 20, and Oliver, 10, also must have walked most of the way. The little party crept north through Massachusetts and into Vermont. They passed through Rutland and pressed on to the eastern shore of Lake Champlain. A ferry took them across the lake to Westport, New York. A day's travel from there put them high in the Adirondacks. John Jr. later called the scenic passage from the Adirondack village of Keene to North Elba "the most grand and beautiful that I ever saw in my life." The trip from Springfield to North Elba took nearly two weeks.

When John, Mary, and the four children got to North Elba, they found Owen, Salmon, and Watson already there. Owen and the two teenagers had driven a herd of Devon cattle up from Connecticut. All the while the rest of Brown's large family were also busy: John Jr. stayed in Springfield to run the wool business. Jason and Frederick were in Akron, Ohio, looking after the sheep-raising end of the Perkins-Brown partnership.

Again, the strong-shouldered patience of Mary Brown must have asserted itself. If her husband's business took her to Franklin Mills, Ohio, she would move there. To Hudson, Ohio. Back to Franklin Mills. To Richfield. To Akron. To Springfield, Massachusetts. Then to what she must have regarded as the North Pole of America: North Elba, New York. She would move temporarily back to Akron for a time when Simon Perkins demanded that Brown be close at hand to look after the firm's failing business. After that, in North Elba, Mary lived for years in what today would be called the worst kind of rural poverty. John Brown was away more than he was home. Most of Mary's small income came from the occasional sale of fleece from the flock of sheep. If the little girls could make a few dollars picking berries for a neighbor, there was joy in the house.

In North Elba, New York, Mary Anne Day Brown did her best to survive on a small farm. Meanwhile, her husband, John Brown, was out doing his best to change the course of history for the entire United States.

# CHAPTER SIX

## On to Pottawatomie

Today thousands of tourists visit the John Brown Farm every summer. The old community of North Elba, New York, has faded off the map into history. Tourists go first to the bustling resort town of Lake Placid, then drive a few miles southeast. There the small Brown family farmhouse still stands, weathered gray-brown by the years and rich in silent memories.

The house belongs to the 1850s. In the large downstairs room,

On and off during much of the 1850s, members of the Brown family lived in poverty in this North Elba farmhouse.

the visitor can almost see John Brown leading his family in morning or evening prayer. Bible in hand, he liked to stand behind a straight chair with a very high back. He would lean forward on this chair, so that its rear legs rose slightly from the floor. At other times in the day, Mary would sit in a corner of the room spinning wool. Three times a day, the all-purpose table was loaded with simple but healthful food. Poor as they were, the Browns usually ate well. African American guests or hired help sat at this table on an equal basis with the Browns. In the 1850s, this was not the usual practice. Neither was the way John Brown talked to his black neighbors. A passing stranger who shared a meal with the Browns and two black people made a diary note on June 28, 1849: "Mr. Brown said a solemn grace. I observed that he called the Negroes by their surnames, with the prefixes of Mr. and Mrs. The man was 'Mr. Jefferson,' and the woman 'Mrs. Wait.'"

Most of the poor black farmers in Timbucto had been cheated on their land. They were helpless when North Elba natives claimed acres that Gerrit Smith had rightfully given the black community. John Brown had no patience with local white people who would do such a thing. He used his surveying skills to redraw property lines to the Blacks' advantage. On Sundays, he served as minister to a small black congregation. With the help of Owen, Salmon, and Watson, he worked his own land as a demonstration farm for his black friends.

John Brown could never spend as much time in North Elba as he would have liked. First, late in 1849, came the sorry trip to England. And then, after his return, the fading fortunes of Perkins & Brown kept him on the road much of the time. From Ohio to Massachusetts, he had to deal with angry sheep farmers, consult with lawyers, and appear in court after court. It would be 1854 before his disastrous partnership with Simon Perkins came to a formal end.

Still, busy as he was, John Brown never forgot the cause of enslaved Americans. Even while away in England he did what he could. He took a short side trip to France, Belgium, and Germany. There he learned all he could about armies and military matters. In Belgium, he visited the famous battlefield of Waterloo, where the French conqueror Napoleon Bonaparte had finally been

**59**

defeated in 1815. John Brown wanted to know how wars were fought and won.

It makes quite a picture: The 49-year-old John Brown wandering around on the great Waterloo battleground. Here the mighty armies of Europe had dug in to fight the greatest battle in history. Here, years later, in this foreign land, the lean, powerful, hardened figure of a Yankee tourist named John Brown wandered the battlefield with the English version of a Waterloo guidebook in his gnarled and callused hand. Beneath graying reddish-brown hair that tended to spike straight up, Brown's eyes would have squinted to take in every detail. As he walked around, stumbling at times, he probably wore his usual brown frock coat, the tails now dancing in a cool September breeze.

Shortly after John Brown's return to his Springfield office, the slavery question in the United States reached a new degree of heat. Many Northerners were alarmed that the vast lands of the Southwest, recently conquered from Mexico, would be turned into slave states. Many Southerners were bitter about the growing economic and political power of the North, which served as a haven for the increasing number of enslaved people escaping northward.

After much debate, Congress passed a series of laws that came to be known as the Compromise of 1850. California was admitted as a free state but the rest of the southwestern territory was organized without mentioning slavery. When that land would eventually be divided into states, these states could be admitted to the Union "with or without slavery, as their [state] constitution may prescribe at the time of their admission." The Compromise of 1850 also settled a Texas–New Mexico border dispute and forbade the slave trade in the District of Columbia but allowed slavery to continue there.

An additional part of the Compromise of 1850 was something Southern slave states had wanted for years. This was a runaway slave law with sharp teeth. The Fugitive Slave Law of 1850 made catching runaway slaves a *federal* responsibility. In every Northern state, special commissioners were appointed to see that enslaved people who had escaped were caught, jailed, and hurried off to certain punishment at the hands of their Southern

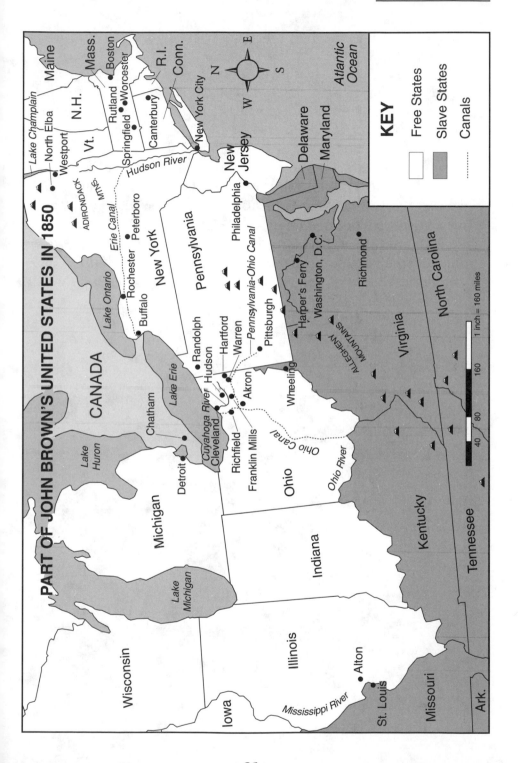

PART OF JOHN BROWN'S UNITED STATES IN 1850

KEY

| | |
|---|---|
| | Free States |
| | Slave States |
| | Canals |

1 inch = 160 miles

40  80  160

Atlantic Ocean

Maine
N.H.
Vt.
Mass.
Boston
Worcester
Rutland
Springfield
Canterbury
R.I.
Conn.
New York City
Lake Champlain
North Elba
Westport
ADIRONDACK MTS.
Erie Canal
Peterboro
Rochester
Buffalo
New York
Hudson River
New Jersey
Delaware
Maryland
Pennsylvania
Philadelphia
Pennsylvania-Ohio Canal
Pittsburgh
Harper's Ferry
Washington, D.C.
Richmond
Virginia
North Carolina
ALLEGHENY MOUNTAINS
Lake Ontario
CANADA
Lake Erie
Chatham
Lake Huron
Detroit
Michigan
Lake Michigan
Wisconsin
Iowa
Illinois
Alton
St. Louis
Missouri
Ark.
Mississippi River
Indiana
Ohio
Ohio Canal
Ohio River
Kentucky
Tennessee
Randolph
Hudson
Hartford
Warren
Akron
Wheeling
Cuyahoga River
Cleveland
Richfield
Franklin Mills

N  E  S  W

masters. Federal marshals could call on anyone they chose to help enforce the law, and refusal to help was a federal crime. People who refused to help could be fined $1,000, at that time equal to several years' wages of a skilled craftsperson. Those who prevented the arrest of a fleeing enslaved person, or assisted in hiding him or her, could also be fined $1,000 and thrown into jail. They could be sued for even more money. Black people accused of being runaways were denied a trial by jury and were not even allowed to speak in their own defense. On the other hand, the word of the slave owner, even if absent, was to be accepted by the commissioners.

The Fugitive Slave Law enraged the abolitionists. It even angered many ordinary citizens who were neutral, or didn't much care, about slavery. When it came to deciding what to do with

To arouse opposition to slavery, abolitionists printed pictures such as this one, showing a slave catcher dragging a woman away.

enslaved people who had escaped from their masters, the federal government was no longer neutral but definitely on the side of the slaveholder. Upon penalty of law, every Northern citizen could be made a slave catcher. Tempers in the North rose even higher when thousands of federal troops were called on to "protect" so-called runaways until their forced return to Southern soil. Moreover, the hundreds of thousands of free African Americans who lived in the North were in danger of being accused of being escaped slaves. Unscrupulous slave catchers could claim these Blacks were slaves, grab them, and ship them South into slavery.

In a few Northern cities, angry mobs stormed police stations and jails, attempting to free black persons held under the new law. But in John Brown's opinion, such acts were far too few. Again Brown was sickened by all the useless talk. Huge candlelight meetings, endless speeches, appeals to the conscience of the South—all these Brown thought useless. Action was called for. And action was what Brown preached to the black community of Springfield, Massachusetts. Even free Blacks there were finding it hard to sleep through the night.

John Brown called a meeting of Springfield's black people. There he presented a long paper he called "Words of Advice." The advice was to form a secret league to protect the rights of African Americans. They should arm themselves. If any Black was arrested, they should attack with overpowering force at once.

> *Do not delay one moment after you are ready; you will lose all resolution if you do. Let the first blow be the signal for all to engage; and when engaged do not do your work by halves, but make clean work of your enemies. . . .* A lasso might possibly be applied to a slave-catcher for once with good effect. . . . *Stand by one another and by your friends, while a drop of blood remains; and be hanged, if you must, but tell no tales out of school. Make no confession.*

All this is typical of Brown: The small group cooperating with no one else. The secrecy. The sudden, surprising armed attack.

The Reverend Theodore Parker had this warning poster printed
in Boston. Parker later became a supporter of John Brown.

The belief that the enemy will back down if it means a fight to the death. And in this case, Brown's plan proved a good one. Forty-four African Americans signed their names to his proposal. Not a single Springfield black person was ever arrested under the Fugitive Slave Law.

John Brown had to write his "Words of Advice" at night, for he was hard at work day after day. The lingering death of Perkins & Brown kept him busy for years. Meanwhile, life for the Brown family had to go on. Brown's daughter Ruth married a young North Elba farmer, Henry Thompson. When business matters kept Brown too long with Simon Perkins in Akron, Ohio, his family finally joined him. The two older sons, John Jr. and Jason, got married, took up small Ohio farms of their own, and started families. Not until 1854 was John Brown free to turn to North Elba and other projects. Once again business failure had left him a penniless man. He hadn't the money even to start a money-raising drive for his Appalachian Mountain scheme.

Two other events also happened in 1854. They are connected in an interesting way.

First, after bitter debate, Congress passed the ill-fated Kansas-Nebraska Act. This law was another compromise between North and South on the question of slavery in new states as the nation expanded westward. The old Missouri Compromise had forbidden slavery in the huge Louisiana Purchase north of the 36°30´ line. The Kansas-Nebraska Act of 1854 repealed that 1820 compromise. The new law was based, instead, on the idea called popular sovereignty. Under this new plan, the people living in a territory ready for statehood would themselves vote slavery up or down. The Kansas-Nebraska Act divided much of what was left of the old Louisiana Purchase into two large new territories: One was the Nebraska Territory, which was west of Minnesota and Iowa and extended all the way north to Canada. The other was the Kansas Territory, west of the slave state of Missouri.

Kansas Territory, everyone knew, was where the hot question of slavery would strike next. Just opened up for settlement, Kansas was attracting more and more homesteaders every day. Before too long a vote would be taken as the territory prepared for statehood. Would Kansas, in the very heart of America,

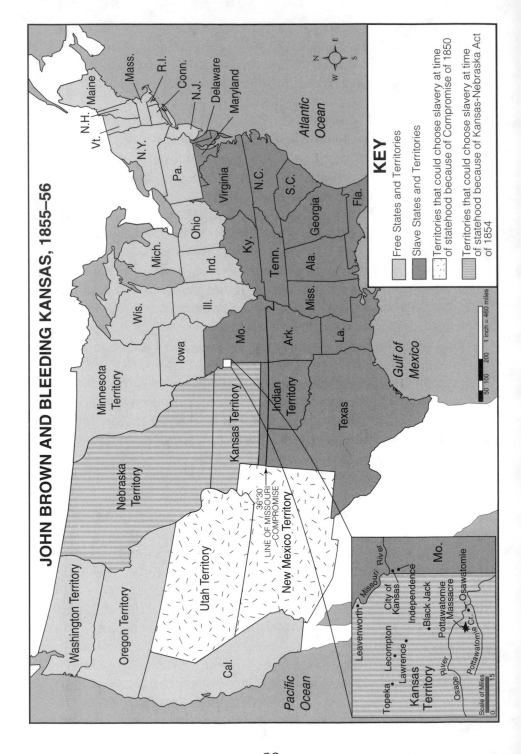

JOHN BROWN AND BLEEDING KANSAS, 1855–56

KEY

Free States and Territories

Slave States and Territories

Territories that could choose slavery at time of statehood because of Compromise of 1850

Territories that could choose slavery at time of statehood because of Kansas-Nebraska Act of 1854

1 inch = 460 miles

50  100  200

Atlantic Ocean

Pacific Ocean

Gulf of Mexico

Maine
N.H.
Vt.
Mass.
R.I.
Conn.
N.J.
Delaware
Maryland
N.Y.
Pa.
Ohio
Mich.
Ind.
Wis.
Ill.
Iowa
Minnesota Territory
Mo.
Virginia
N.C.
S.C.
Ky.
Tenn.
Georgia
Ala.
Miss.
Fla.
Ark.
La.
Texas
Indian Territory
Kansas Territory
Nebraska Territory
Washington Territory
Oregon Territory
Utah Territory
New Mexico Territory
Cal.

LINE OF MISSOURI COMPROMISE
36°30'

Missouri River

Leavenworth
City of Kansas
Independence
Mo.
Lecompton
Lawrence
Black Jack
Topeka
Pottawatomie Massacre
Osawatomie
Kansas Territory
Osage River
Pottawatomie Cr.

Scale of Miles
0  15

66

become a free state? Or would it be a sister to the slave states in the South?

Kansas was now up for grabs, and both North and South reached out with eager hands. Organizations were formed in both North and South to encourage people to resettle there. Kansas was advertised as the new American paradise. There huge farms could be claimed on government land. The cost was only $1.25 an acre, money that could be paid years later. Eastern Kansas was gently rolling country with rich soil. The many rivers and streams were bordered by woodland.

Also in 1854 came the worst drought in Ohio history. John Jr. and Jason saw their corn spring green from the ground, turn yellow, and then dead brown as no rain fell for weeks on end. By midsummer it was clear that the crop would be lost. Farmers all over Ohio were suffering. When John Brown learned of his sons' hardships, he said that the Lord must be punishing a guilty land. After all, what had the people of Ohio done about the sin of slavery on their southern doorstep in Kentucky and Virginia?

By this time in their lives, John Jr. and Jason had abandoned their father's rigid religious beliefs. Their reactions to the drought were more practical. Ohio was a disaster area. The Kansas Territory was being billed as the land of milk and honey. In the old Brown tradition, the two young farmers decided to pull up stakes and try life somewhere else. They had little trouble persuading Owen, Frederick, and Salmon Brown to join them. Even 16-year-old Oliver made plans to leave for Kansas. This left only Watson at home to help John Brown on the North Elba farm.

By the spring of 1855, five of the Brown brothers—John Jr. and Jason with their families, as well as Owen, Frederick, and Salmon—had reached eastern Kansas with their farm animals and equipment. The brothers claimed large tracts of land 12 miles northwest of Osawatomie, a town near the meeting of the Osage River and Pottawatomie Creek. It was good farmland in beautiful country. Thinking of future generations, they called their settlement Brownsville (or sometimes Browns' Station).

The lush farmland pleased the Browns. But they were not at all pleased by the political situation. Most settlers from the North wanted to make Kansas a free state for free people. Most settlers

**67**

From five of his sons who had moved to Kansas Territory, John Brown learned firsthand about the conflict over slavery there.

from the South, whether they owned slaves or not, wanted to win Kansas for slavery. The two groups eyed each other with suspicion. Each group tended to stick together. For the most part, they founded their own towns. They shopped in their own stores. They read their own Kansas newspapers. When John Jr. passed through a slave-state settlement, he felt he was in an enemy area. He wondered if and when open warfare would break out. Both sides wanted desperately to win the forthcoming vote for representatives to the territory's legislature, which would decide whether or not the new state of Kansas would permit slavery within its borders.

So far, the local elections in Kansas had not gone well for free-state settlers. Most Kansas voters lived within a long day's ride of the Missouri border to the east. Missouri was a slave state. When an election was to be held, thousands of Missouri men would rush into Kansas like a holiday army. Soon called Border Ruffians, they brought Bowie knives and rifles. They often brought cannons, sometimes brass bands, and always bottles of whiskey. The Missourians would insist they were residents of Kansas and entitled to vote. If refused, they terrorized and even tortured voting officials. In November 1854, it took 2,000 Border Ruffians to elect a proslavery territorial delegate to the U.S. Congress. The following March, 5,000 Missourians gave Kansas Territory a legislature that supported slavery 38 to 1.

In May 1855, John Jr. wrote a long letter to his father in North Elba. He told about the Border Ruffians and the fight for Kansas. The slave-state people, he said, were well armed. The South intended to win Kansas by fraud and force. Unfortunately, the free-state settlers had few weapons. Now, it was said, an army of 3,000 was forming in Missouri to drive out of Kansas "every Anti Slavery man they can find in it . . . *now* while they can nip their opponents in the bud." John Jr. reported that free-state men were forming a militia, or citizens' army. But they lacked everything from Bowie knives to muskets, rifles to cannons. "Now we want you to get for us these arms," John Jr. pleaded. "We need them more than we do bread."

John Brown could not resist his son's appeal. The struggle over slavery, it was clear, now centered on Kansas. He would send all the arms he could. More than that, he would go to Kansas himself.

As soon as he could, John Brown left North Elba, New York, for Brownsville, Kansas. With him went his young son-in-law, Henry Thompson. On the trip Brown went out of his way to speak before every antislavery group he could find, pleading for support. He was disappointed in the money raised, but the weapons began to pile up. In Illinois, they joined up with Oliver Brown, who had stopped to work there on his way to Kansas.

Brown was going to Kansas to fight, not to farm, and he had no time to waste. The shortest route to eastern Kansas lay across the slave state of Missouri—and this, Brown knew, would be a problem. Missourians often gave pioneers with Northern accents a troubling time. Brown dared not take a Missouri River steamboat across the state. His boxes would probably be examined. If he was found to be a Northerner carrying arms, his life might be in danger. Instead, he decided to cross Missouri with a one-horse wagon. In the bottom of the wagon were the boxes of weapons. On top was his surveying equipment in full view. That way, he hoped, he, Oliver, and Henry Thompson would look like a surveying team. Most surveyors heading for Kansas had been hired by the federal government, which supported the proslavery Kansas Territory legislature.

The three travelers made it, but not without strain. The horse grew sick. It could walk only 8 or 10 miles a day, even with the three men trudging beside the wagon to lighten the load. There were threats: "You'll never live to get thar." Some farm families refused to give the horse a pail of water. Near Independence, Brown saw a slave pen and auction block. He saw groups of black people in chains, handled worse than cattle headed for slaughter. Nearing the Kansas border, Brown heard Border Ruffians boast that they wouldn't let up until every last abolitionist in Kansas was either running away or dead.

When Brown finally reached Brownsville, he was down to his last 60 cents. Even worse, he was shocked at what he saw. John Jr. and Jason, their wives and small children, and also Owen, Frederick, and Salmon—nearly all of them—were ill with a malarial fever. It was early October; winter was approaching, yet his family was still living in tents. Their new farm was in poor condition. John Jr. and Jason had spent much time away on free-state business. The rest, growing sick with fever, hadn't been able to manage.

If the family situation upset John Brown, so did the political one. The "bogus legislature," as free-state people called it, had met in July 1855. Its first laws were aimed straight at the abolitionists. To speak against slavery could mean a term in jail. Possession of abolitionist literature could bring years behind bars. Of course, actually helping an enslaved person escape would trigger the death penalty. The "bogus legislature" had pulled no punches.

In response, many antislavery settlers had claimed that the proslavery government was illegal. They drew up their own constitution, called the Topeka Constitution, which they adopted by popular vote in December 1855. Within a month, they elected an antislavery governor and legislature to rival the proslavery ones. But the federal government refused to recognize the antislavery territorial government, which continued anyway as a sort of "shadow government."

Meanwhile, John Brown's first job had been to get his family healthy once again and ready for winter. Then he turned his attention to that "greatest or principal object." Daring local proslavery officials to arrest him, he went around saying that he not only considered the black man a brother but would fight for his rights. He was spoiling for a fight. But where, and when, would the shooting start? The government was in the hands of proslavery officials. Groups of Border Ruffians ranged here and there. Threats were common. Now and then a free-state settler would be shot, but the free-staters could do little about it. This angered John Brown. He wanted action.

Brown finally got his chance about two months after his arrival in Kansas. A free-state man was shot dead. The government arrested not the killer but a friend of the victim, whose only crime was uttering threats against the murderer. The arrested man was to be taken to Lecompton, the proslavery center, by an armed guard. But on the way, an antislavery posse rescued the man and took him to Lawrence, the free-state center. Soon an army of 2,000 Border Ruffians was camped outside Lawrence, waiting for a chance to show that the only good abolitionist was a dead one.

John Brown and his sons turned a farm wagon into a small fort on wheels. Traveling through the December night, they hurried to help in the defense of Lawrence, about 30 miles to the north. They arrived to a grateful welcome. Their new supply of weapons passed into eager hands. This older man and leader, this gaunt and serious John Brown, certainly seemed to know what he was talking about. Almost at once he was made a captain in the Fifth Regiment, First Brigade of Kansas Volunteers.

But there would be no fighting. The territorial governor, Wilson Shannon, arranged a temporary peace between the two sides. The following day, when the peace plan was being explained at a large public meeting, Brown would have none of it. "I spit on it!" he scoffed, leaping up before the ragtag free-state militia. He said he could lead a night raid that would destroy the Border Ruffian army, huge as it was. Only with some force was the excited troublemaker John Brown pulled down and made to shut up.

The following winter was a terrible one. Still living in makeshift shelters, the Browns' battle was now with the snow and the ice and the cold. But by the following May, John Brown was itching for action again. A settler army of 300 men under Major Jefferson Buford had just come from Alabama. No one knew what Buford's Raiders intended to do, but John Brown was sure they were up to no good. Learning that they were camped a little south of Pottawatomie Creek, John Brown set out to investigate. Once again, he used his surveyor's disguise. With two sons as helpers, he took his equipment and began to run lines right through Buford's camp. The trick worked. Salmon Brown heard the Southerners say they would wipe out "those damned Browns" and keep the heat up "until every damned abolitionist was in hell."

On Thursday, May 22, 1856, another cry for help came from Lawrence. Once again, a large proslavery force had found an excuse to threaten the free-state center. The Border Ruffians had now been joined by Buford's Raiders. By this time, John Jr. had

Violence in Kansas, 1856. Proslavery forces attacked Lawrence, burning down its hotel, looting homes, and destroying the offices and presses of antislavery newspapers.

been chosen captain of a small militia group called the Pottawatomie Rifles. John Brown and his sons went along with this group as they left for Lawrence toward evening. But during the night they met a messenger coming south from Lawrence. He had the worst possible news. It was already too late. Lawrence had surrendered without a fight. The free-state headquarters was in flames. Other buildings had been leveled or burned. Drunken looters roamed at will.

According to Salmon Brown, more bad news arrived early the next morning. It too came by messenger. Senator Charles Sumner of Massachusetts, a strong foe of slavery, had nearly been killed on the floor of the U.S. Senate. Congressman Preston Brooks of South Carolina—feeling that a speech by Sumner had insulted the South, his state, and his family—had walked up to Sumner at his Senate desk and started beating him with a cane. Sumner, a very tall man, was unable to rise, cramped in by a desk

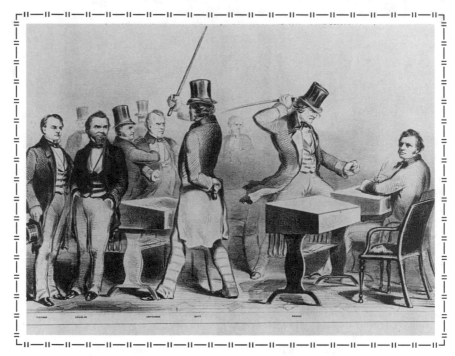

Violence in the U.S. Senate, 1856. Congressman Brooks of South Carolina attacks Senator Sumner of Massachusetts after Sumner called the Kansas-Nebraska Act "in every respect a swindle."

screwed to the floor. The blows grew harder. With blood blinding both eyes, Sumner had at last wrenched the desk upward. But he could not see. When Brooks's cane broke in two, he began using the pointed stick left in his hand as a dagger.

Camped in the wilds of Kansas Territory, John Brown must have felt the blows of "Bully Boy" Brooks as if crashing down on his own head. Something must have snapped in Brown's brooding brain. Was the antislavery battle now lost? The Fugitive Slave Law had made the federal government the slaveholders' servant. Slavery forces had taken Kansas by fraud. Six free-state men had been killed so far. *Lawrence had surrendered without a fight!* Now the force of slavery had even spattered the United States Senate with innocent blood. Something had to be done. *Something.*

About noon, John Brown and several others separated themselves from the Pottawatomie Rifles, who had stopped to eat and rest. Brown's group included four of his sons, Owen, Frederick, Salmon, and Oliver; his son-in-law, Henry Thompson; and two men who lived near Pottawatomie Creek, Theodore Weiner and James Townsley. Soon they were seen sharpening short swords on a grindstone. Then they left, riding off south in Townsley's wagon.

That night the group camped near Pottawatomie Creek. There they waited all the next day. Then, well after dark, they rode on toward a proslavery settlement near the Pottawatomie. The people living there were all ordinary working people. One, a man named Wilkinson, was a member of the "bogus legislature." Some were constables or other local officials. Not one of them owned a single slave. Yet all believed with a passion that slavery had to triumph in Kansas.

The night raiders headed first for the house of a settler from Tennessee, Pleasant Doyle. In the dark of the night, dogs growled, barked, and then rushed forward. Frederick Brown and James Townsley soon silenced the dogs with their swords. Then John Brown and some of his sons burst into the Doyle cabin. The Northern army had come, Brown declared. In a moment, the whole Doyle family stood in the dim light before Brown, trembling in their nightclothes. A little girl. Three young men. Pleasant and Mahala Doyle. Brown ordered the men outside. Mahala Doyle begged him not to take young John, who was only 14. Brown agreed. He marched the other three outside. According to Salmon Brown, Mahala Doyle then said to her husband: "I told you you would get in trouble for all your devilment; and now you see it has come."

The Wilkinson cabin lay about a half mile away. This time Brown's job was easier. The children were all too young. Mrs. Wilkinson said she had measles; she needed someone to stay with her. Allen Wilkinson asked that he at least be allowed to put on his boots. Brown refused both requests. Wilkinson was marched out into the windy May night.

Brown's party next aroused those in the cabin of James Harris. John Brown knew little about Harris. At gunpoint, the man was taken outside and questioned. Had he ever helped the proslavery people in Kansas? Had he helped destroy Lawrence? Had he ever made threats against free-state settlers? James Harris was released, but John Brown still claimed another victim. Unfortunately, a man named William Sherman had stopped to spend the night at the Harris home. Sherman was the brother of "Dutch Henry" Sherman, a known proslavery loudmouth who scattered threats with every breath. William Sherman was ushered out into a darkening future.

The tragic night did not really end till well after daybreak the following morning. Pleasant Doyle had been stabbed in the chest and shot in the head. Young William Doyle lay beside him with his head cut nearly open. Drury Doyle, who must have tried to run, was found about 100 yards away. He had a wound in his chest and his arms cut off. Allen Wilkinson had suffered multiple stab wounds before he died. William Sherman's body was found beside a brook, with the left hand cut off. The bubbling water was carrying away pieces of brain from an open skull.

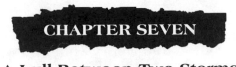

# CHAPTER SEVEN

## A Lull Between Two Storms

News of the Pottawatomie massacre spread like a prairie fire. People for miles around were seized in the hard fist of fear. Would slave-state hotheads seek sudden revenge? Would the Browns strike again. Who would be next?

By the time John Brown's gang of cutthroats made it back to the Pottawatomie Rifles, everyone in east-central Kansas seemed to know about the crimes. There was little doubt that the Browns were guilty; John Brown was easy to identify, and there were several witnesses. Jason Brown asked his father at once if his group had killed the Pottawatomie settlers. Yes, John Brown replied. And furthermore, he, John Brown, was responsible for the whole thing.

"Then you have committed a very wicked crime," Jason said.

"God is my judge," John Brown stated.

Strangely, it was John Jr. and Jason, the two Brown brothers who had had nothing to do with the crimes, who suffered most. John Jr. gave up his leadership of the Pottawatomie Rifles and went into hiding in the wild. Dreadful fears slowly took over his mind. When a band of Border Ruffians picked him up, he had lost his senses. He was brutally tortured, given scars he would bear the rest of his life. Then he was marched off to Lecompton for three months in jail.

Jason chose a more sensible course. He decided to surrender to the U.S. Army and try to explain that he had done nothing wrong. But before he could find an army unit, the Border Ruffians found him. He was nearly hanged, but spared at the last minute. He, too, was brutally treated, but not tortured. He, too, was jailed, but let go after a short time. Meanwhile, the families of John Jr. and Jason had sought shelter in a friendly house near Osawatomie. Behind them, Brownsville was burned to the ground.

Captain Brown (as John Brown was now commonly called), Owen, Salmon, Oliver, and Henry Thompson were of course marked men. With a few other free-state roughnecks, they took to the wild and lived like outlaws. For food and supplies, they raided slave-state stores and settlements. (This is the origin of the label "horse thief" that John Brown's enemies often applied to him.) Soon Brown learned that a force led by Henry Clay Pate, a deputy U.S. marshal, was out to get him. In typical Brown fashion, he decided to strike first. On the morning of June 2, 1856, Brown's band attacked Pate's men as they were eating breakfast at a place called Black Jack. It was rough, wooded country, just the kind of place Brown liked for a battle. Although outnumbered more than two to one, Brown's men used bravery, bluffing, and a bit of luck to win the day. Pate surrendered with 21 men. The "Battle of Black Jack" first brought Brown's name to nationwide attention.

After Black Jack, one by one, the Browns began to tire of Kansas. There were several reasons for this. After all, they could

Bleeding Kansas, 1856. Free-state forces in Kansas Territory received weapons from abolitionists to fight slave-state forces.

not go on living a hungry and filthy outlaw life forever. Sooner or later, they would be killed or jailed. Also, the federal government was now making a real effort to force all private armies out of Bleeding Kansas, as people now called that violent region. Both Border Ruffians and free-state private armies were being forced to yield power to the U.S. Army. Moreover, the now-famous "sack of Lawrence" had brought a huge new wave of support from Northern states. New free-state settlers, well armed and financed, were pouring into Kansas every day. Finally, John Brown began to wonder what—or *whom*—he was really fighting for. The new free-state constitution, drawn up by the shadow government and approved by free-state voters, not only banned slavery in the territory but also banned all black people. John Brown had absolutely no wish to fight for someone else's dream of a "lily-white" Kansas.

By the middle of the summer, Owen, Salmon, Oliver, and Henry Thompson had left for the East. The rest decided to wait for John Jr.'s release from prison in mid-September. But John Brown was not a man to sit idly by. He could not resist one parting shot.

In late August 1856, Brown learned that a new army from Missouri had entered Kansas Territory in a last-minute effort to drive the free-staters out for good. One part of this Missouri army, under a man named John W. Reid, was now nearing Osawatomie with orders to level the place. Captain John Brown, with a force swelled by volunteers to 30 men, determined to do all he could. For a time, Reid's 300 troops moved this way and that around Osawatomie. Brown had to know what was going on. He sent his son Frederick out as a scout. Frederick carried no gun and tried to act like an innocent civilian. About a mile from Osawatomie, he encountered a small detachment of Reid's forces. Among them he spotted one Martin White, a local man who was acting as a guide. Approaching White, Frederick asked, "Don't I know you?"

"I know you," replied White, "and you are my enemy."

White then raised his gun and fired. Frederick fell to the ground, a bullet through his heart.

News of Frederick's death must have sent needles of fury

79

An 1856 photo of John Brown. After the brutal Pottawatomie massacre, the mention of his name spread terror in Kansas.

coursing through John Brown's body. Outnumbered 10 to 1, Brown could not take on Reid's army directly. He stationed his force in some woods that lay parallel to Reid's line of march. When the massed enemy passed by, the free-staters' guns exploded. Brown's men fought like devils—even Jason Brown, who found a new courage he had never felt before. But at last, with a third of his men killed or badly wounded, Brown had to retreat.

A short time later, John Brown and his bedraggled band stood on a low hill overlooking Osawatomie. The whole town was going up in flames. There were tears in Brown's eyes. "God sees it," he told his son Jason. He did not yet know that his stand at Osawatomie would make him a hero in the eyes of many. He had come to like the sound of "Captain Brown." Soon he would be signing his name "Osawatomie Brown."

When Brown left Bleeding Kansas about a month later, he did not hurry home to North Elba. He lingered in Iowa and then in Ohio. The reason would become clear to others later. Already, he was working out the details of his secret plan for the grand invasion of the Southern mountains, the elaborate plan he had presented to Frederick Douglass years earlier. Brown decided to start by seizing a U.S. arsenal at Harper's Ferry, Virginia. While not revealing the plan, he did tell a reporter that they were now living through "a treacherous lull before the storm. We are on the eve of one of the greatest wars in history."

John Brown would never spend much time in North Elba again. He was always on the move, getting money and weapons for his "greatest or principal object." Since he was subject to arrest, he sometimes used a false name such as Shubel Morgan or Isaac Smith. Also during this period, he started to grow the flowing white beard of the later heroic portraits. At times, he had to go into hiding. At other times, depending on circumstances, he would appear quite openly as the old Kansas fighter, Osawatomie Brown.

When asked about the Pottawatomie massacre, Brown would usually say something like, well, the killings had not really been a bad idea or he would feel proud to have ordered them himself. Hadn't the massacre made hundreds of proslavery settlers pack

**81**

up and scramble out of Kansas? Brown always made it very clear that he had killed absolutely no one himself. This was, in a strict sense, true. Until after the Civil War, Brown's part in the Pottawatomie killings was a matter of rumor only. Not until about 1880 did it become reasonably clear that he had been the man in charge but left the actual bloodletting up to his sons.

Little by little, Brown built up a network of antislavery supporters with money and influence. The most important of this group later became famous as the Secret Six. The wealthy Gerrit Smith of Peterboro, New York, was a long-time backer. Thomas

Theodore Parker, famous theologian, scholar, abolitionist, and social reformer, was one of the Secret Six.

Wentworth Higginson of Worcester, Massachusetts, was a coura-geous minister, active in many fields. Another minister, Theodore Parker of Boston, may have been both the country's most popu-lar preacher and its most learned man. Another Bostonian, Dr. Samuel Gridley Howe, was famous for the education of the visu-ally and hearing impaired, the insane, and the mentally handi-capped. From the Boston area, too, came George Luther Stearns, who had made a fortune in the linseed-oil business, and Franklin Sanborn, a young teacher and writer.

When speaking to a general audience, Brown would never mention Harper's Ferry or even the Virginia mountains. The sur-prise attack had to be kept secret. Instead, after telling hair-rais-ing tales of Black Jack and Osawatomie, he would appeal for money and arms, for new violence he said was sure to break out in Kansas. The Secret Six knew differently, of course. So would anyone who followed Brown's actions, rather than his words. In March 1857, for instance, a Connecticut blacksmith named Charles Blair heard Brown speak and talked to him afterward. Brown then placed an order for 1,000 pikes with Blair. (A pike was a razor-sharp, double-edged steel blade attached to a wooden pole about five and a half feet long.) What good would pikes have been against well-armed Border Ruffians in Kansas? Weren't pikes better suited for Southern slaves who had never fired a gun and in whose hands firearms were sure to be dangerous?

Charles Blair may have thought about these questions. Or he may have believed that true wisdom lay in lack of thought. Even the Secret Six had their doubts when they thought too hard upon the matter. Would Brown's amazing plan for the Southern moun-tains really work? Not one of the Secret Six was really sure. One thing they were sure of, however: Brown would proceed with or without their help. Thus, they felt they had no choice. Not helping might mean sending Brown to a certain death. Better not to think about it. "I do not wish to know Captain Brown's plans," Gerrit Smith wrote to another. "I hope he will keep them to himself."

By the end of 1857, John Brown had accomplished a great deal. He had hired Hugh Forbes, a British soldier of fortune and the author of a military book. Forbes had begun to train the small beginnings of a liberation army. Brown also had access to 200

Hugh Forbes was a military expert whom Brown hired to train his army of liberation. Forbes wrote a training manual for the troops.

rifles and 200 revolvers, although these were supposed to be used only in Kansas. He was awaiting the delivery of the 1,000 pikes he had ordered. In early 1858, he spent three weeks with the great black leader Frederick Douglass in Rochester, New York. When not talking to Douglass, Brown spent most of his time writing a "Provisional Constitution for the People of the United States." This document was to serve as basic law for the separate government in the Allegheny Mountains, the name of a section of the long Appalachian mountain chain that included the Harper's Ferry region. A simpler version of the U.S. Constitution, it outlawed slavery and laid claim to the property of slave owners and those who agreed with them.

To formally approve the document, Brown called for a constitutional convention in May 1858. He chose the Canadian town of Chatham, near the north shore of Lake Erie, not far from Detroit. There were many Blacks in that area who had fled the United States, and Brown wanted their support. Many of the 36 who attended seemed interested. (But in the end Brown was to be disappointed. Only one African American from Canada actually came to take part in the Harper's Ferry raid.)

In Chatham, for the first time, John Brown revealed his true plans to a sizable number of people. Now he felt he had to take some chances. He needed a volunteer army, and he needed it fast. His complicated plan—involving money, arms, and men—called for Harper's Ferry to be attacked in the fall.

Then disaster struck. Hugh Forbes, who had suffered under Brown's "I-know-everything" attitude, had already quit in disgust. Forbes, a military man, had liked the mountain plan. But he thought that even with Brown's hoped-for 80 or 100 men, Brown did not have the strength to pull off the Harper's Ferry plan. Now it seemed that Forbes was in Washington, D.C., talking about Brown's Virginia mountain plan with top politicians. The Secret Six, fearing for their own hides, panicked at once. Brown had always told the public that Kansas was his goal—and now, the Secret Six said, to Kansas he must go. There was no time to waste. Brown must make some kind of a major diversion in Kansas to draw the Washington dogs off whatever scent Forbes had given them. If it was very clear that Brown was again in Kansas, Forbes's amazing stories would be laughed away as the work of a crackpot.

Brown returned to Kansas to find the shock of another massacre still in the air. A private Southern army had rounded up several free-state men, taken them to a quiet spot, opened fire, and left them for dead. But, in fact, only five were killed, another five wounded. Brown announced he was in Kansas to guard the dangerous Missouri border. However, nothing happened. (In fact, the battle over Kansas was now over. There would be no more massacres. Free-state settlers could now beat proslavery voters six to one at the polls. Not until 1861, however, would Kansas be admitted to the Union as a free state.) While in Kansas Territory, Brown came down with ague, the malarial fever that had troubled him in the past. He lay in bed for four weeks. When he recovered, he went back to guarding the Missouri line. Things were as quiet as before—much too quiet for a troublemaker like John Brown.

In December, one of John Brown's men met a Missouri black man near the border who had a sorrowful tale. He, his wife, and his children were enslaved people who were about to be sold to separate buyers. The family would be broken up. What could be done? Was there anyone in Kansas who would help James Daniels and his family?

John Brown could not resist. The next night two Missouri slaveholders were awakened to a living nightmare. When one of them seemed too trigger-happy, he was shot and killed. The Daniels family was liberated. So were seven other Blacks who wanted to go along. So were horses, oxen, clothes, and a wagon full of the best food.

Hiding the escaping Blacks when necessary and moving with utmost care, Brown made his way to Osawatomie, to Lawrence, and then north to the Nebraska Territory border. The group usually traveled at night and hid during daylight hours. Over and over, Brown risked his life to make local sheriffs and U.S. marshals fear for theirs. Things became easier when the party crossed the Nebraska Territory–Iowa line into the free state of Iowa. There Brown sometimes spoke at meetings under his own name. With nearly white hair and a long, white, flowing beard, he seemed a gnarled oak of a man who could laugh at lightning. He cut a commanding figure. People who described him tended to add two or three inches to his height. He was openly breaking the Fugitive Slave Law and getting away with it. He was defying all the mighty power of the U.S. government.

From eastern Iowa, the Daniels family and the others escaping from slavery were transported to Detroit by railroad boxcar. From there, it was only a short water crossing to Canada and freedom. The trip had covered 1,100 miles and taken three months. Now it was time for Brown to return to North Elba.

Of course, John Brown did not stay there long. He had to arrange the shipment of firearms and pikes. He had to meet with the Secret Six. Most of the Secret Six, he was glad to learn, now thought that the original plan could get back on track.

By midsummer of 1859, John Brown, disguised as an old Yankee farmer named Isaac Smith, was walking the streets of Harper's Ferry, Virginia. The North was too cold for him now, he told people. He had sold out and wanted to try farming in Virginia. In July, he rented the Kennedy farm in Maryland, about six miles north of Harper's Ferry.

One of Brown's men, John Cook, had already been working in Harper's Ferry for a whole year, scouting the area. Brown's sons Owen and Oliver were already with him. Watson Brown came soon, bringing along from North Elba two brothers of Henry Thompson. In the weeks that followed, more men would trickle in from across the North. Two were from Canada: a white man named Stewart Taylor and a black man named Osborn Anderson.

In 1859, Brown grew his famous biblical-looking beard that was to become part of the image of John Brown as martyr.

Some of the antislavery force had fought with Brown in Kansas; others he had never met before. Some were highly educated, others could hardly sign their names. A total of five from the whole group were African Americans.

Like John Brown, all the men hated slavery enough to risk their lives in a fight to end it. Beyond that common purpose, they were as different as any group that might have been put together. Some were out for fame and glory. Others wanted to find only peace in the hands of God. Only one had an immediate interest in what he was about to do. This was the tall, distinguished-looking Dangerfield Newby.

Dangerfield Newby, hoping to free his wife, joined forces with John Brown.

Dangerfield Newby, at 48, was the oldest of Brown's soldiers. He had spent most of his life in slavery about 40 miles beyond Harper's Ferry. He had a wife, Harriet, and seven children. Then his white master—who was also his real father—had died. The dead man's will had made Newby a free man. But it was illegal for a freed black person to stay on and work in Virginia. Newby had gone north to the nearest free state, Pennsylvania, where he worked as a hired man. He had planned to buy his wife and children out of slavery—but in fact, this was impossible. His pay was so low, and the price of slaves so high, that Newby could have labored the rest of his life in vain. When he heard of John Brown's plan, he saw it as his only hope to join Harriet once again. Dangerfield Newby always carried Harriet's latest letter in his pocket. Now she said that her master needed money. She might be sold. "Oh dear Dangerfield, com this fall without fail monny or no Monney I want to see you so much that is the one bright hope I have before me."

Unfortunately, the Kennedy farmhouse was within sight of the road. There were neighbors. Brown's men had to keep quiet and out of sight. They spent most of their time huddled together in the hot attic. There they studied the small military book that had been written for the group by Hugh Forbes. They read and reread the Provisional Constitution. They polished their rifles. They assembled the 1,000 pikes, which had been shipped in pieces as hoe handles and kitchen knives. But mostly there was nothing to do. Arguments started. Tempers flared. Thunderstorms always came as a great relief, for then the men could shout, sing, dance, and stamp on the floor without risk of being heard.

John Brown grew worried. He sent to North Elba for his 16-year-old daughter, Anne (now called Annie), and Oliver's young bride of 17, Martha. There were trains, now, all the way from northern New York to southern Pennsylvania. The young women came at once. They posed as Isaac Smith's daughters. Their very presence had an uplifting and quieting effect on the men. Although they cooked and did some housework, their greatest help was in handling curious neighbors. Sitting on the porch, Annie would signal the men inside the house, when someone

**89**

The Kennedy farmhouse in Maryland was the planning center for John Brown's attack on nearby Harper's Ferry.

walked up the driveway. If the person entered and looked too long at the many boxes of firearms and ammunition, Annie or Martha would say that the crates contained the family furniture. Their mother, Mrs. Isaac Smith, was a very particular woman. The girls had been forbidden to open the crates before she arrived.

Still, Brown's worries grew. Once, open rebellion broke out within the group. Some of the men, including Brown's own sons, were overcome by doubt and fear. The Harper's Ferry project was an impossible idea. Why not abandon it now and save a lot of lives? John Brown again insisted that his plan would work. Moreover, it would work well, without the shedding of very much blood. In a clever move, John Brown suddenly resigned as their leader and went outside. When he returned, he found that his trick had worked. The movement was too far advanced for anyone to quit now and leave the others hanging by a thinner thread. The men would stick together—out of loyalty to old Osawatomie Brown if for no other reason.

Brown's worries continued to mount as July turned into August. John Jr., still shaken by his Kansas horrors, had refused to head for Harper's Ferry. He had, however, volunteered to work full-time getting weapons and men to Brown's small army. So far, he had done a good job with the firearms. They had been shipped by rail to Chambersburg, Pennsylvania. From there they had been hauled 50 miles by wagon to the Kennedy farmhouse. But what about the men? Brown had once counted on 80 or 100. Now he had only about 20. In desperation, Brown kept writing to John Jr. What about the promises of support from black leaders like J. W. Logan and Henry Highland Garnet? What about Frederick Douglass?

John Brown wanted to see Douglass personally. He set up a meeting toward the end of August. The two men held their secret conference in an old stone quarry near Chambersburg. Brown was disguised as a fisherman. Both he and Douglass brought a man along as a guard. They talked—or, rather, argued—for most of two days. In their viewpoints, both were as hard and unmoving as the blocks of stone they sat upon.

Brown's aim was to get Douglass to join him. According to Brown, when news spread that the greatest black leader in the United States was at Harper's Ferry, Blacks who had been enslaved would come running from all directions. "Come with me, Douglass," Brown asked. "I will defend you with my life. I want you for a special purpose. When I strike, the bees will begin to swarm, and I shall want you to help hive them."

Douglass would have none of it. He was generally sympathetic to Brown's mountain plan. But, he later said, he told Brown that in striking at Harper's Ferry he would be "going into a perfect steel-trap, and that once in he would never get out alive." No, Brown argued. Harper's Ferry was absolutely necessary. If he just went quietly into the Virginia mountains, how would the slaves know he was there? Who would believe it? No, he had to begin with a blow whose ringing echo would be heard everywhere. Harper's Ferry would be big news. Moreover, he would take several important people as hostages. If worst came to worst, he could use the hostages as bargaining chips to get his men safely into the Virginia mountains.

Nonsense, said Douglass. He told Brown that Virginia would "blow him and his hostages sky-high, rather than that he should hold Harper's Ferry an hour."

Brown would not abandon his plan. Douglass would not go along. "He regretted my decision and we parted," Douglass finished his account of his last meeting with John Brown.

As September became October, Annie and Martha were sent home to North Elba. The time was drawing near. But Brown had only about 20 men. Where were all the rest who had said they would come? At the last minute, Brown went to Philadelphia with his top lieutenant, John Kagi. There he met with black leaders and white abolitionists. He sadly discovered that their once-promised courage now meant nothing. Brown returned to the farmhouse near Harper's Ferry.

On the morning of October 16, 1859, John Brown, as he did every day, honored God with prayer and Bible readings. The day passed with nerves at full stretch. The men cleaned their rifles. They reviewed the Provisional Constitution for still another time. They tried to get a little sleep. They went over their individual instructions. Finally, they ate their last supper together. Almost as soon as it got dark, John Brown barked the order:

"Men, get on your arms. We will proceed to the Ferry."

# CHAPTER EIGHT

## On to Harper's Ferry

Harper's Ferry is now in West Virginia, but there was no state of West Virginia in 1859. The northwestern section of old Virginia, whose people had little interest in slavery and stayed loyal to the Union, split off from Virginia during the Civil War in 1863 and formed a separate state. But then as now, Harper's Ferry lies between two rivers, like an arrowhead pointed east. On the "top" side runs the Potomac River, which forms the boundary with Maryland to the north. On the "bottom" is the Shenandoah River, which runs into the Potomac River at the very tip of the Harper's Ferry arrow.

Harper's Ferry, (West) Virginia, was a small town settled in about 1747 and the site of a U.S. arsenal established in 1796.

In 1859, the town had about 2,000 people. The livelihoods of nearly all of them depended on the manufacture, storage, and transportation of weapons for the U.S. government. Next to the Potomac was a long row of buildings called the armory. Here muskets had been manufactured for years. A railroad from Wheeling, (West) Virginia, to Baltimore, Maryland, ran past the armory and crossed the Potomac into Maryland through a covered bridge at the point where the two rivers met. Near the bridge was what was called the arsenal, a three-story brick building for the storage of weapons. A half mile up the Shenandoah, past a plank bridge over the river, was Hall's Rifle Works, a large arms factory.

John Cook, Brown's scout in Harper's Ferry for a year, had been pleased to find that although the town produced weapons for the army, there were no army units stationed there. The bridges and important buildings were guarded by only a civilian watchman or two. Basically, Harper's Ferry was just another small, sleepy American town. Many of the workers had come south to Virginia from Springfield, Massachusetts, another arms center. Cook said that the only personal weapons the people owned were an occasional squirrel rifle or small revolver.

A little before 10 o'clock on the night of October 16, 1859, 19 men descended from the Maryland heights overlooking Harper's Ferry. (Three had been left behind to guard the weapons in the Kennedy farmhouse and bring them down later.) Their leader, old Osawatomie Brown, rode in a wagon most of the way. The rest walked through a light drizzle, gray scarfs thrown over the rifles on their backs.

As they neared the Potomac bridge, the two men in front, John Cook and Charles Tidd, cut the telegraph wires that connected Harper's Ferry to the outside world. The guard on the bridge was an easy prisoner. The men trudged on beside the railroad track that led through the long covered bridge. On the other side, it was as if the town itself were asleep. Even the Galt House, a saloon to the left, seemed to be snoring. Straight ahead was the huge brick arsenal. To the right was a building that was both the train station and the Wager House, a hotel and restaurant. Beyond it was the armory. That was Brown's destination.

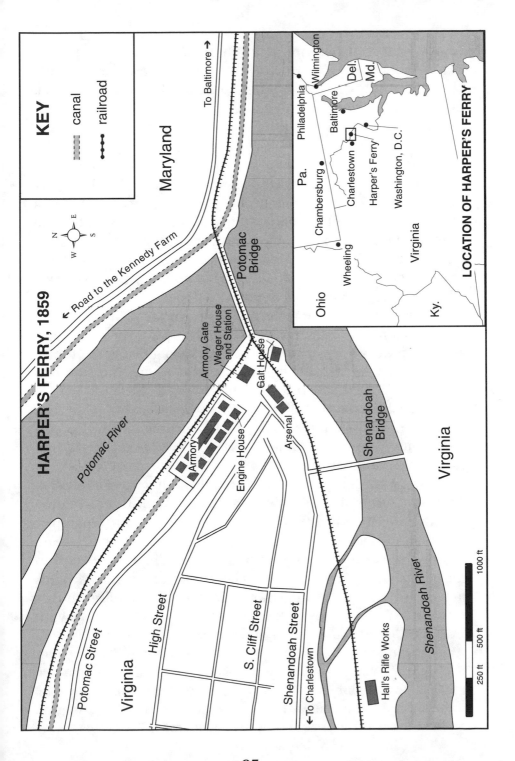

## HARPER'S FERRY, 1859

### KEY

canal

railroad

N
W — E
S

Maryland

← Road to the Kennedy Farm

To Baltimore →

Potomac River

Potomac Bridge

Armory Gate
Wager House and Station
Galt House

Armory

Engine House

Arsenal

Shenandoah Bridge

High Street

S. Cliff Street

Shenandoah Street

Potomac Street

Virginia

← To Charlestown

Hall's Rifle Works

Shenandoah River

Virginia

250 ft   500 ft   1000 ft

### LOCATION OF HARPER'S FERRY

Wilmington

Del.

Md.

Philadelphia

Baltimore

Pa.

Charlestown

Harper's Ferry

Washington, D.C.

Chambersburg

Wheeling

Ohio

Virginia

Ky.

The first of the armory buildings was called the Engine House. Today the building would be called a firehouse. It contained firefighting vehicles and equipment. Brown had already selected it as his headquarters. Centrally located, it had thick brick walls and three massive oak doors. With no low windows, it made a perfect small fort. In front of it was a tall iron gate, part of the fence that enclosed the whole armory area.

A lone watchman had been sitting by a stove in another room at the rear of the Engine House. Hearing Brown's wagon rumbling near on the cobblestone street, he now came forward. Brown's men were already climbing the fence and leaping over. No, the watchman would not open the gate. Even with guns held against his head and chest, he could not manage to produce a key. Then one of Brown's men brought a crowbar from the wagon. He used it to snap the chain that held the gate closed. The bridge guard and the watchman became the first of Brown's 40 hostages.

The plan had been gone over so many times that now it seemed to work on its own. Two men were to guard the Potomac bridge. Two others went to the Shenandoah bridge. Three went to guard the arsenal. Brown himself led a small group up Shenandoah Street to Hall's Rifle Works. There he left John Kagi, his second in command, in charge. Then he marched back to his command post at the Engine House. The townspeople were still asleep and unsuspecting.

About midnight, six of Brown's men left on a special mission. They were to go five miles west to the home of Colonel Lewis Washington, the most notable man in the area. Washington, a great-grandnephew of George Washington, was to be Brown's prize hostage. He was an officer in the state militia and an aide to the governor of Virginia. Two special treats were planned for this handsome example of Virginia's white upper crust. First, it was well known that his most-loved possession was a dress sword worn by George Washington on ceremonial occasions. Colonel Washington would be ordered to present this sword in surrender to Osborn Anderson, a black man. Second, Washington would be told that although he was a prisoner, all his slaves were now free. If they wanted, the liberated people could help guard Washington on the return to Harper's Ferry. Other just-freed Blacks there were

96

to wake up all their friends for miles around and tell them to hurry to Harper's Ferry.

Also about midnight, the first shot was fired. A civilian guard named Higgins had walked toward the Potomac bridge, ready to begin his shift. But something was wrong. The light at the end of the bridge had been put out. And where was the other guard he had come to relieve? Soon he was face to face with Oliver Brown and William Thompson. Higgins resisted capture. They scuffled. When Oliver Brown seemed in danger, Thompson fired. The bullet just grazed Higgins's head as he ran away.

This was a direct violation of Captain Brown's orders. Brown had said over and over that Harper's Ferry could be taken "without very much blood." No one was to fire until it was absolutely

Osborn Anderson, a printer, came from Canada to help John Brown in his 1859 raid on Harper's Ferry.

necessary. Now a slightly wounded man was free to alert the sleeping town. Moreover, the gunfire had awakened other people who lived nearby. Before too long, one of them would be riding through the night to the nearest large town—a latter-day Paul Revere screaming for the Charlestown (now Charles Town) militia to wake up and grab their muskets.

At one-thirty, a mail train headed for Baltimore came chugging up the tracks along the Potomac. It carried a few passengers. Higgins, whose scalp wound was not serious, dashed out to warn the engineer. The conductor hopped off, along with some passengers. Shephard Hayward, a free black man who worked as a baggage handler at the station, joined the group. The conductor didn't know what to make of Higgins's strange story. Except for the bridge light being out, Harper's Ferry looked just as it always had. He led the other men toward the bridge, just to take a look.

There in front of them were Oliver Brown and William Thompson, with rifles as pointed and directed as their eyes. Trigger-happy once again, Thompson fired a warning shot in the air. The group turned and ran. Thompson fired another shot, and this time the bullet passed through the body of Shephard Hayward. He staggered and fell. Someone managed to drag him into the station office. There he died.

A strange happening: The first person to be fatally wounded in the Harper's Ferry raid was a free black man. Shephard Hayward was a hard-working, responsible man, well liked in the community. He had a family. He was shot in the back while trying to flee.

The night passed without further gunfire. A sizable group had gathered in the Wager House and station, but no one knew what to do. Brown may have guessed that men were speeding to nearby towns as fast as their horses could gallop. But in the quiet of the night, John Brown knew that he owned Harper's Ferry. At times his men would lead in another hostage. These were people like old Mr. Grist, picked up on the Shenandoah bridge on his way home from a church meeting.

The light rain had continued, on and off, throughout the night. Dim lanterns had provided the only light. Now, as the sky began to brighten, the pace of activity picked up. The superintendent of all government works at Harper's Ferry, alerted at his home, appeared at the armory gate to ask what was going on. As with his other hostages, John Brown was most courteous.

Brown was unfailingly polite to all his hostages. He told them who he was and why he was there. He apologized for the inconvenience. He hoped it would not last long. Some hostages were allowed to go home briefly, under guard, to calm any fears their families might have. Later, at breakfast time, Brown ordered huge meals sent over from the Wager House kitchen. Those hostages not too nervous to eat, or not too suspicious of poison in the food, enjoyed ham, hot cakes, eggs, and plenty of coffee.

Just as it was getting light enough to see, a clatter was heard coming up the cobblestone street. It was Colonel Lewis Washington, under the guard of Blacks, in his fancy carriage. Another vehicle, a sturdy four-horse wagon, carried about 10 liberated people. In addition, it also contained another Virginia aristocrat, named John Allstadt, at whose place the night raiders had also stopped. In a little ceremony that seemed to delight Brown, those just freed were given pikes to fight for their new freedom.

John Brown was especially pleased to see the big four-horse wagon. He ordered three of his men and four liberated slaves to take the wagon across the Potomac to the Kennedy farm. There they were to get the remaining pikes, rifles, and revolvers. John Cook, who was in charge of the party, told Brown that he hoped to return with an army of at least 150 Maryland slaves. Like the first trip to Colonel Washington's, this trip was supposed to sound the great bell of freedom. The men were also to pick up another wealthy slaveholder, a man named Terence Byrne. Brown still had great faith that such people were the best hostages and his surest protection.

At this point, John Brown made the decision to let the train proceed on toward Baltimore. First, he got the conductor's promise to keep the events in Harper's Ferry a secret. But at the very next stop, the conductor went running to the telegraph office. Soon telegraph lines across the nation were sizzling with a mixture of facts, rumors, and the conductor's worst fears. "NEGRO INSURRECTION AT HARPER'S FERRY, VIRGINIA . . . SEVEN HUNDRED AND FIFTY BLACK AND WHITE ABOLITIONISTS HOLD ARSENAL AND GUN WORKS . . . THE

John Kagi, named by John Brown as his secretary of war and second in command, took over Hall's Rifle Works at Harper's Ferry.

NAME OF THE LEADER IS OSAWATOMIE BROWN . . . BROWN EXPECTS REINFORCEMENTS OF FIFTEEN HUNDRED MEN BY TOMORROW MORNING . . ."

At Harper's Ferry, the morning passed quietly. But it was a quiet that oozed with cold sweat and tension. It was *too* quiet. This was an armed rebellion; yet for the time being, it was silent suspense. Now and then Brown's men traded gunfire with a courageous civilian. One local man was killed. From his post at Hall's Rifle Works near the Shenandoah bridge, John Kagi kept sending Brown messages. When was Brown coming? Wasn't it time to get across the Shenandoah bridge and into the Virginia mountains? Why the delay? According to Osborn Anderson, the black raider who had received George Washington's sword, Brown "appeared somewhat puzzled." All morning Brown had expected to see slaves coming on the run to join his forces. Where were they?

Meanwhile, things were quiet. Brown still had his hostages for protection. He did nothing.

About noon there came a great stir on the other side of the Potomac bridge. Brown uttered a cry of joy. Cook had arrived with his Maryland army! But gunfire suddenly filled the air, and the men then on guard—Oliver Brown, Stewart Taylor, and Dangerfield Newby—came running out of the covered bridge. It wasn't Cook's armed Blacks. It was the militia, the Jefferson Guards from Charlestown. The militiamen poured through the bridge, then stopped in confusion as they faced a hail of bullets from Brown's men. The militia retreated into the bridge, but in the moments that followed, Dangerfield Newby was hit by a civilian sniper. It wasn't just a bullet; it was an iron spike that tore his neck apart.

Another strange happening: The first of Brown's men to be killed was a free black man, Dangerfield Newby. He lay in a pool of blood in the gutter long after he was dead. Later in the afternoon, someone dashed out and cut off his ears as souvenirs.

The rest of the afternoon was a disorganized disgrace. The Galt House saloon and the barroom in the Wager House did a brisk business. As militiamen from other towns arrived, they seemed more interested in occupying the bars than the Engine House. By this time, Brown had selected his 11 most important hostages to stay with his group in the Engine House. The rest, along with some confused black men holding pikes, huddled in the watchmen's room to the rear. Outside, the drunken mob screamed for John Brown's blood. They splattered the Engine House with musket fire that did little harm. It was hard to get a shot through the thin crack made when one of the doors opened from time to time to return fire.

Brown remained remarkably calm. When one of his men wanted to use the hostages as human shields, to force an escape, he would have none of it. But now, he realized, the time had come to use the hostages as bargaining chips. He would make a deal. Reason Cross, one of the hostages, agreed to carry Brown's terms to the mayor of Harper's Ferry. Brown would release the

**101**

hostages in return for a cease-fire until the arrival of U.S. troops—everyone assumed they were on the way—who would settle all disputes.

Reason Cross and Brown's man William Thompson left the Engine House, a white handkerchief tied to Thompson's gun. The mob honored the white flag. They did not shoot. But suddenly Thompson was seized and carried off. Brown had no way of knowing that soon Thompson would be shot at point-blank range and thrown off the Potomac bridge. Neither did John Brown know that what he considered a reasonable offer would be met with howls of laughter. The mob wanted dead abolitionists. No deal.

Nor could Brown know what would soon happen to other of his men. Will Leeman, his youngest fighter, tried to get across the Potomac to spur on the force on the other side. He was shot dead by pursuers. Then his body was propped up against some rocks in the middle of the river. Drunken militiamen used it for target practice all afternoon. At Hall's Rifle Works, John Kagi and two others knew they had no chance against an approaching mob of hundreds. They splashed into the Shenandoah, trying to flee. Two, including Kagi, were shot dead, one captured.

Brown tried to deal again. This time another hostage went out

Oliver and Martha Brown. Oliver was killed at Harper's Ferry.

John Brown Jr. did not take part in the raid at Harper's Ferry.

under a flag of truce with Watson Brown and Aaron Stevens. Brown's two men were shot. His son Watson managed to crawl back to the Engine House, where he would lie dying a slow death. Late in the afternoon Oliver Brown was hit by a lucky bullet that found its way through a crack in the Engine House door. He joined his brother Watson in dying agony on the floor. The emotion that now must have surged through John Brown can only be imagined. Both of Brown's sons had young wives back in North Elba. Oliver's bride was pregnant. Watson had a baby son he had not yet seen.

Still Brown wanted to strike a bargain. This time he dealt through an older civilian who walked back and forth with a white handkerchief tied to the tip of a raised umbrella. Brown wanted back his surviving men and also his horses. In return for them and for the chance to escape, he would take the hostages across the Potomac bridge a little way. Then he would let them go. The answer came back soon: again, no deal. Brown's plea for a doctor to treat his wounded sons went unanswered.

About dark, a man approached the Engine House and wanted entry. Brown thought that, at last, it might be a doctor. The man turned out to be a newcomer on the scene, a Captain Sinn of the Frederick, Maryland, militia. He informed Brown that 90 United

Owen Brown was able to escape from Harper's Ferry.

Watson Brown was shot to death at Harper's Ferry.

**103**

States Marines and some regular army officers had just arrived. Brown's situation was hopeless. He had only four able men with him now in the Engine House. Why not give up? Brown said no; he repeated his surrender terms. Sinn explained that the drunken mob was out of control, and so there was no way Brown and his men could walk safely to the Potomac bridge. Then Sinn left. Later he sent a doctor attached to his unit to look at Watson and Oliver. During the long night, Oliver died.

The first light of morning revealed that U.S. Marines were, in fact, in charge of Harper's Ferry. By special orders from Washington, D.C., they were under the command of U.S. Army Colonel Robert E. Lee. Lee first sent a junior officer, J. E. B. Stuart, to the Engine House under a flag of truce. Stuart and Brown talked a long time. Then Stuart left, jumping out of the way and signaling with his hat to Lee.

Almost at once the U.S. Marines stormed the Engine House. Using a heavy ladder as a battering ram, they finally broke one of the sturdy oak doors. They poured in. Because of the hostages in the room, they had orders not to shoot. Two of Brown's men were killed with bayonets. The U.S. Marine in charge, Lieutenant Israel Green, went after Brown himself with a sword. He managed to cut old Osawatomie, but Green's final, mighty, killing thrust must have hit Brown's belt buckle. The sword blade doubled over, useless. Brown's life was spared.

The final tally at Harper's Ferry in terms of lives lost: 1 U.S. Marine, 2 slaves, 4 civilians, and 10 of Brown's raiders—including Watson Brown, who died of his wounds the day after the raid ended. Seven of the raiders, including Brown himself, were later given a trial and executed. Five, including Owen Brown and Osborn Anderson, escaped to safety in the North and were never punished.

Salmon Brown, who had refused to take part in the raid, wrote later: "We never learned just how father accounted for his being trapped as he was." No one has ever managed to solve this puzzle. Perhaps Brown really thought that with the hostages he could bluff his way to safety. Perhaps he thought his cause was better served by a dead martyr than by a doomed man in the mountains. Perhaps his disappointment that many enslaved

U.S. Marines storm the Engine House. This engraving was based on a sketch made on the spot by a magazine artist.

people did not come running to join in the fight paralyzed him.

It is much easier to explain *why* those people stayed away. Very simply put, Harper's Ferry was a horrible idea from the start. Hugh Forbes had said so. Frederick Douglass had said so. Brown's own sons had said so. The enslaved Blacks had a wisdom far more on the mark than John Brown's dreams. No slave rebellion in the United States had ever succeeded. No black rebellion had ever been led by a white man. From past experience, the Blacks had learned it was the white man who tried to trick the slaves, who set traps, who started rumors to show up at a certain place and time. Enslaved black people in the South knew the horrors in store for rebelling slaves who were caught.

It is often said, "not one slave came running to join Brown's rebellion." This is untrue. A slave at Colonel Washington's, missed

105

when the raiders were there, did come running to catch up at the Allstadt house. No one knows how many slaves hung around the edges of Harper's Ferry, waiting to see what would happen. And some of the slaves freed by Brown's raiders showed remarkable courage. On the tailgate of the four-horse wagon that left Harper's Ferry for the Kennedy farm sat a big black man with Colonel Washington's best shotgun across his knees. The fire in the eyes of that scowling face struck terror into all white people who saw it, and was remembered long afterward.

# CHAPTER NINE

## "A Bright Morning . . . A Glorious Day"

As the blood stains spread on John Brown's clothing, he was dragged outside the Engine House. Surrounded by U.S. Marines, he lay as if dead. The crowd screamed with lynch-mob fury. Then Brown raised his head and looked around. Amazingly, his many wounds were not fatal. For his own protection, he was carried to the paymaster's office in the armory. Someone got some old bedding and threw it down on the floor. There Brown collapsed and passed out. It was Tuesday morning, and he had not slept since Saturday night.

Wounded prisoner John Brown in the Harper's Ferry armory. This sketch was made at the time by a news magazine's artist.

When John Brown began to come to, early in the afternoon, the room was filling with people: the army officers Robert E. Lee and J. E. B. Stuart, Governor Henry A. Wise of Virginia, Senator James M. Mason of that state, Colonel Lewis Washington, some congressmen, a few reporters, some important citizens who had managed to talk their way into the small room. All crowded around to get a glimpse of old Osawatomie, who lay covered by a blanket, his head against the back of an overturned chair. His hair was the color of clotted blood. On his face there was also blood which had run down into his recently trimmed grizzly beard.

Robert E. Lee introduced officials like Governor Wise and Senator Mason. Did the prisoner want the others to leave the room? No, Brown said, he welcomed the chance to make his actions completely understood. Undoubtedly he was glad to see the reporters already scribbling in their notebooks. He had lost the battle of Harper's Ferry. But now, he saw, he had won a page-one place in newspapers across the nation. He took every possible advantage.

Then, for three hours, John Brown put on the performance of his life. He spoke carefully and thoughtfully, with well-chosen words. Next day's newspapers (Wednesday, October 19, 1859) reported with equal care. Here are a few examples:

SENATOR MASON: Can you tell us who furnished money for your expedition?

JOHN BROWN: I furnished most of it myself; I cannot implicate [involve] others. It is by my own folly that I have been taken. I could easily have saved myself from it, had I exercised my own better judgment rather than yielded to my feelings. . . . I should have gone away; but I had thirty odd prisoners, whose wives and daughters were in tears for their safety, and I felt for them.

MASON: If you would tell us who sent you here,—who provided the means,—that would be information of some value.

BROWN: I will answer freely and faithfully about what concerns myself,—I will answer anything I can with honor,—but not about others.

MASON: What was your object in coming?

BROWN: We came to free the slaves, and only that.

A VOLUNTEER: How many men, in all, had you?

BROWN: I came to Virginia with eighteen men only, besides myself.

VOLUNTEER: What in the world did you suppose you could do here in Virginia with that amount of men?

BROWN: Young man, I do not wish to discuss that question here.

VOLUNTEER: You could not do anything.

BROWN: Well, perhaps your ideas and mine on military subjects would differ materially.

MASON: How do you justify your acts?

BROWN: I think, my friend, you are guilty of a great wrong against God and humanity,—I say it without wishing to be offensive,—and it would be perfectly right for any one to interfere with you so far as to free these you wilfully and wickedly hold in bondage. I do not say this insultingly.

MASON: I understand that.

BROWN: I think I did right, and that others will do right who interfere with you at any time and at all times. I hold that the Golden Rule, "Do unto others as ye would that others should do unto you," applies to all who would help others to gain their liberty.

LIEUTENANT STUART: But don't you believe in the Bible?

BROWN: Certainly I do.

MASON: What wages did you offer?

BROWN: None.

STUART: "The wages of sin is death."

BROWN: I would not have made such a remark to you if you had been a prisoner, and wounded, in my hands.

REPORTER: I do not wish to annoy you; but if you have anything further you would like to say, I will report it.

BROWN: I have nothing to say, only that I claim to be here in carrying out a measure I believe perfectly justifiable, . . . to aid those suffering a great wrong. I wish to say furthermore, that you had better—all you people at the South—prepare yourselves for a settlement of this question, that must come up for settlement sooner than you are prepared for it. The sooner you are prepared the better. You may dispose of me very easily,—I am nearly disposed of now; but this question is still to be settled,—this Negro question I mean; the end of that is not yet. . . .

The following day John Brown was taken under heavy guard to the county jail in Charlestown, where the courthouse was also located. The state of Virginia wanted to hang him as soon as possible. The countryside still trembled with unknown fears. Mysterious fires kept breaking out, and rumors ran riot. People worried that a force from Boston was on its way to free John Brown. Especially since Brown sounded so reasonable, it was hard to believe he had really invaded Virginia with only 18 men. The real abolitionist army, it was said, hundreds if not thousands strong, was marching south.

Only a week went by before the trial began. Again, John Brown used every advantage. He was the star of the show; he knew what he said was the news of the day. He knew courtroom artists were constantly at work, making drawings as he lay on a

John Brown in the courtroom. This sketch was made 40 years after the event. Note the inaccurately depicted long beard.

cot before judge and jury. When, despite the physical pain, he propped himself up on one elbow and raised his voice, he could score point after point. "If you seek my blood," he announced at the start, "you can have it any moment without the mockery of a trial. . . . I am ready for my fate. I do not ask a trial."

At first, Brown made many protests. He said he was too weak to stand trial. He claimed that he did not have good lawyers and that those he did have lacked time to prepare the case. But in the end, Brown said he felt "entirely satisfied with the treatment I have received on my trial. Considering all the circumstances, it has been more generous than I expected." In truth, Brown was represented by good lawyers, both court-appointed attorneys and volunteers from the North. In the Virginia of late 1859, no team of lawyers could have kept John Brown's neck from the noose. He was clearly guilty of the charges of murder and inciting slaves to rebel. These were both death-penalty crimes according to the Virginia law at the time. His main defense was that things had not gone as planned. "I never did intend murder, or treason, or the destruction of property, or to incite or excite slaves to rebellion, or to make insurrection [revolt]." The jury was not impressed. Regardless of Brown's *intent*, the jury thought, the crimes charged against him had taken place.

At the end of the trial, John Brown was asked if he had anything to say. Again, he took every advantage. He rose from his cot and on uncertain legs stood before the judge. He reminded the court that a year earlier he had liberated slaves in Missouri and had taken them to Canada. The Harper's Ferry raid, he said, was to be "the same thing again, on a larger scale." Then, pointing to the Bible used to swear in witnesses, Brown said,

> I see a book kissed here which I suppose to be the Bible, or at least the New Testament. That teaches me that all things whatsoever I would that men should do to me, I should do even so to them. It teaches me, further, to "remember them that are in bonds, as bound with them." I endeavored to act up to that instruction. I say, I am yet too young to understand that God is any respecter of persons. I believe that to

**111**

have interfered as I have done—as I have always freely admitted I have done—in behalf of His despised poor, was not wrong, but right. Now, if it is deemed necessary that I should forfeit my life for the furtherance of the ends of justice, and mingle my blood further with the blood of my children and with the blood of millions in this slave country whose rights are disregarded by wicked, cruel, and unjust enactments,—I submit; so let it be done!

On November 2, 1859, John Brown was sentenced to hang by the neck until dead. The date of execution was to be a month away, December 2.

John Brown made the most of that month. He was kept locked in his cell in the Charlestown jail, but he was a busy man.

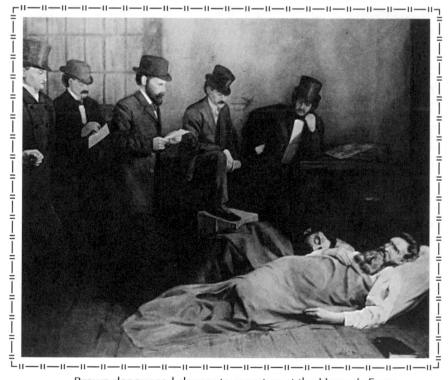

Brown denounced slavery to reporters at the Harper's Ferry armory, in court, and even in jail while awaiting execution.

The Virginia authorities allowed him to see a steady stream of visitors. He wrote letter after letter. In nearly all of them, he said he was "quite cheerful." He was filled with "the peace of God, which passeth all understanding." True, his Harper's Ferry plan had failed, but that had been his own plan, not God's plan. Now he believed that God's plan had called for him to fail. His defeat and death would do more to free the slaves than success at Harper's Ferry could ever have done. "I think I cannot now better serve the cause I love than to die for it, and in my death I may do more than in my life." He "would not walk out of the prison if the door was left open." In his last letter to his wife, John Brown rejoiced "in the certain & near approach of a bright *Morning,* & a *glorious day.*"

Mary Brown made two requests. She wanted to see her husband before he died, and she wanted to take the body back to North Elba for burial. The state of Virginia said yes to both pleas. Mary Brown arrived on December 1 and shared her husband's last supper.

John Brown now wanted to hang. It was part of God's plan for the unfolding future. He would die a brave man. He had told the authorities that he did *not* want one of the slaveholders' so-called Christian ministers uttering prayers at the gallows. Instead, he would have preferred "that my only *religious attendants* be poor *little, dirty, ragged bare headed, & barefooted Slave boys; & Girls;* led by some old *grey headed Slave Mother.*"

Friday, December 2, 1859, was a warm, sunny day. John Brown started the morning reading his Bible for a long time. Then he wrote Mary a note about what he wanted chiseled into his tombstone at North Elba. About eleven o'clock he was taken from the jail to a waiting wagon. In the wagon was his coffin, now to be his seat on the ride to the gallows.

There is a famous painting of a heroic John Brown on the jailhouse steps, bending down to kiss a slave child. This picture is an artist's version of the spirit of John Brown. The truth was quite different. Brown still wore his ragged Harper's Ferry clothes. An old, wide-brimmed hat was pulled low on his head. His beard was short and scraggly. With guards at his sides and marched between two rows of armed soldiers, there was no way Brown

This dramatic, moving, but historically inaccurate painting
is the "Last Moments of John Brown" by Thomas Hovenden.

could have got near a black child. Indeed, everywhere he looked there were armed men. Fifteen hundred soldiers filled the streets of Charlestown and the nearby field where Brown was to hang.

On the way to the gallows, John Brown lifted his eyes to the gentle, rolling farmland and the Blue Ridge Mountains beyond. "This *is* a beautiful country," he said to his guard. "I never had the pleasure of seeing it before." Arriving at the gallows, he walked up the steps without hesitation. He took his place on the trapdoor. Then, with the noose around his neck and a white hood over his head, he was forced to stand still for 10 minutes. The officer in charge insisted on waiting until all the troops on duty were lined up in their assigned places.

Finally the soldiers were in formation. The signal was given. The sheriff aimed a sharp axe at the rope that held the trapdoor.

John Brown, about to be executed by hanging, December 2, 1859.
The sketch was made on the spot by a newspaper artist.

Brown dropped until the noose snapped his neck. The body jerked, then hung still. "So perish all such enemies of Virginia!" boomed the colonel in charge. "All such enemies of the Union! All such foes of the human race!"

That was one announcement. Another was contained in a note Brown had handed one of his guards just before leaving the jail. It was written in his usual neat, carefully underlined handwriting:

> CHARLESTOWN, VA, 2D. DECEMBER, 1859
> I John Brown am now quite <u>certain</u> that the crimes of this <u>guilty, land: will</u> never be purged <u>away</u>; but with Blood. I had <u>as I now think: vainly</u> flattered myself that without <u>very much</u> bloodshed: it might be done.

Harper's Ferry meant many things to many people. In Virginia, Harriet Newby was sold off to a slave dealer from Louisiana. In New York, Gerrit Smith was led off to a mental hospital, waving his arms and shouting that he was headed for Virginia to help John Brown. Others of the Secret Six panicked when they learned that Brown had clumsily left evidence in the Kennedy farmhouse involving them. Samuel Gridley Howe, George Luther Stearns, and Franklin Sanborn hurried to Canada. Theodore Parker, having traveled to Italy for his health, breathed a sigh of relief that he was already out of the country. Of the Secret Six, only the brave minister Thomas Wentworth Higginson refused to destroy letters, deny the truth of his involvement with Brown, or flee the imagined claws of the law—which, in fact, never even scratched any of the six conspirators.

But in a larger sense, Harper's Ferry meant an end to the compromise that had long held North and South together. Some respected voices in the North insisted on making Brown a saint. In Concord, Massachusetts, the poet and essayist Ralph Waldo Emerson called Brown "that new saint who will make the gallows glorious like the Cross." While almost no Northerners approved of the raid itself, many people said they could understand *why* Brown had acted as he did. It was this repeated understanding of

**116**

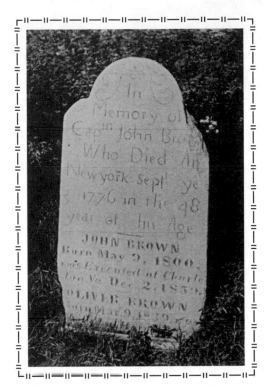

John Brown's grave, North Elba, New York.

the *why* that so angered the South. Southerners began to believe that the abolitionists could—and would—take over the country. Exactly a year after John Brown's death, the Southern states began to leave the Union. Four months after that, the first shot of the Civil War was fired at Fort Sumter in South Carolina. By the end of the war four years later, over 600,000 more people had died. But John Brown's dream was a fact at last. Four million enslaved people were free.

Union soldiers, as they marched from battle to battle during those long years of war, often sang of the spirit they felt marching beside them. There are several versions of the song; this probably comes close to the original:

John Brown's body lies a-moldering in the grave,
While weep the sons of bondage whom he ventured all to
   save;
But though he lost his life while struggling for the slave,
His soul is marching on.
   Glory, glory hallelujah!
   Glory, glory hallelujah!
   Glory, glory hallelujah!
   His soul is marching on!

| | |
|---|---|
| **1800** | John Brown is born in Torrington, Connecticut, the son of tanner Owen Brown and Ruth Mills Brown. |
| **1805** | The Brown family moves to Hudson, Ohio, where Owen Brown becomes a homesteader and continues his tanning business. |
| **1816-17** | John Brown's effort to study for the ministry in the East is abandoned because of failing eyesight and lack of funds. |
| **1820** | John Brown and Dianthe Lusk marry. |
| **1825-35** | Brown operates a tannery in Randolph, Pennsylvania. |
| **1832** | Dianthe Brown dies. |
| **1833** | John Brown and Mary Anne Day marry. |
| **1837** | Brown publicly dedicates his life to ending slavery in the United States. |
| **1842** | Years of financial difficulties caused by excessive speculation in land end with a court-approved bankruptcy. |
| **1846** | Brown, now in a sheep-raising partnership with Simon Perkins, opens a wholesale wool business in Springfield, Massachusetts. |
| **1847** | John Brown discusses his plan to establish a slave-liberation army in the Southern mountains with black abolitionist Frederick Douglass. |
| **1849** | The wool business fails with a disastrous trip to England. Brown moves his family to North Elba, New York, where he hopes to assist a community of African American homesteaders. |

| | |
|---|---|
| **1855** | Brown goes to Kansas Territory to help the anti-slavery forces. |
| **1856** | Brown is responsible for the Pottawatomie massacre and fights heroically at Black Jack and Osawatomie in Kansas. |
| **1859** | As the first step in his grand Southern-mountain plan to free the slaves, Brown raids Harper's Ferry, (West) Virginia. After his small force is crushed, he is tried, convicted, and sent to the gallows. |

**abolitionist** A social reformer who spoke out against slavery and worked to end it.

**academy** A school usually above the elementary level, especially a private high school

**armory** A place where arms such as guns and other weapons are manufactured.

**arsenal** An arms storage center.

**bankruptcy** The legal process by which a person or company that cannot pay its debts has a court decide how the person or company's financial matters should be run to pay off the money owed or how the remaining property should be distributed among those to whom money is owed. Once the process is complete, the person or company is legally free of past debts.

**constable** A public officer usually of a town, whose job is similar to that of a sheriff, although the constable's powers are less. A constable is responsible for keeping the peace and for minor judicial duties.

**executive order** A rule or regulation issued by the U.S. President for the purpose of carrying out a provision of the Constitution or a law or treaty.

**foundation stock** Livestock of good quality from which one begins breeding a herd.

**marshal** A U.S. marshal is an officer appointed by the U.S. President in each judicial district to execute all lawful U.S. orders and laws in much the same way that a sheriff of a state enforces state laws.

**militia** Temporary citizen-soldiers called for service in emergencies, in contrast to regular troops.

**musket** A heavy, large-caliber, muzzle-loading shoulder gun.

**pike** A heavy spear weapon made of a razor-sharp, double-edged steel blade attached to a long wooden pole.

**popular sovereignty** A pre-Civil War theory that people living in a newly organized territory had the right to decide by vote of their territorial legislature whether or not slavery should be permitted there.

**posse** A group of people usually summoned by a sheriff to help in preserving the public peace, especially in an emergency.

**shanty** A small crudely built house or hut, usually made of wood.

**soldier of fortune** A person who follows a military career, going wherever there is likely to be profit or adventure.

**specie** Coin of precious metals such as gold or silver.

**tannery** A place where animal hides are changed to leather by treatment with tannin-rich bark or other special chemicals.

**theologian** An expert in the study of religious beliefs and practices who has usually undergone specialized religious training.

**treason** The act of betraying one's government by waging war against it or by giving help and comfort to the enemy.

**vagrancy** The act of going about from place to place by a person without visible means of support who is idle and who, though able to work, refuses to do so, but lives without labor or on the charity of others.

**warrant** A legal order. An arrest warrant is an order issued by a court commanding law enforcement officers to arrest a specific person.

# BIBLIOGRAPHY

## AND RECOMMENDED READINGS

Abels, Jules. *Man on Fire: John Brown and the Cause of Liberty.* New York: Macmillan, 1971.

Boyer, Richard O. *The Legend of John Brown: A Biography and a History.* New York: Alfred A. Knopf, 1972.

Du Bois, W. E. Burghardt. *John Brown.* Philadelphia: George W. Jacobs, 1909.

Furnas, J. C. *The Road to Harpers Ferry.* New York: William Sloane Associates, 1959.

*Graham, Lorenz. *John Brown: A Cry for Freedom.* New York: Thomas Y. Crowell, 1980.

*Iger, Eve Marie. *John Brown: His Soul Goes Marching On.* New York: Young Scott Books, 1969.

McPherson, James M. *Battle Cry of Freedom: The Civil War Era.* New York: Oxford University Press, 1988; Ballantine Books, 1989.

Nelson, Truman. *The Old Man: John Brown at Harper's Ferry.* New York: Holt, Rinehart and Winston, 1973.

Oates, Stephen B. *To Purge This Land with Blood: A Biography of John Brown.* New York: Harper & Row, 1970.

Redpath, James. *The Public Life of Capt. John Brown.* Boston: Thayer and Eldridge, 1860.

Ruchames, Louis, ed. *A John Brown Reader.* New York: Abelard-Schuman, 1959.

Sanborn, F. B. *The Life and Letters of John Brown.* Boston: Roberts Brothers, 1885.

*Scott, John Anthony, and Robert Alan Scott. *John Brown of Harper's Ferry.* New York: Facts on File Publications, 1988.

Stavis, Barrie. *John Brown: The Sword and the Word.* New York: A. S. Barnes, 1970.

Villard, Oswald Garrison. *John Brown: 1800-1859. A Biography Fifty Years After.* Boston: Houghton Mifflin, 1910.

*Webb, Robert N. *The Raid on Harpers Ferry, October 16, 1859.* New York: Franklin Watts, 1971.

*Especially recommended for younger readers.

## PLACES TO VISIT

Akron, Ohio
- The John Brown Home is the reconstructed house inhabited by John Brown at different times. It is part of a historical exhibit that features the Perkins Mansion, built by John Brown's financial backer in the wool business, Simon Perkins.

Charles Town, West Virginia (formerly Charlestown, Virginia)
- Here, a short distance from Harpers Ferry, the visitor can see the courthouse where John Brown was tried and convicted, the site of his hanging, even the wagon that transported him to the gallows. The Jefferson County Museum offers samples of Brown-related material.

Harpers Ferry, West Virginia (formerly Harper's Ferry, Virginia)
- The Harpers Ferry National Historic Park contains the restored 19th-century village and many other reminders of John Brown's famous raid in 1859. Exhibits include museums and the rebuilt Engine House where Brown made his last stand.

123

| | |
|---|---|
| Lake Placid, New York (near former community of North Elba) | • At the John Brown Farm Historic Site in the old community of North Elba, the visitor can see John Brown's last house and his grave. Tombstones also honor Brown's sons and others killed in the antislavery struggle. The remains of Dangerfield Newby, the African American who was the first raider shot at Harpers Ferry, were removed to this site in 1899. |
| New Richmond Township, Pennsylvania (location of what was once Randolph) | • In New Richmond Township near Route 77 are the remaining foundation walls of the John Brown Tannery. Nearby are the graves of John Brown's first wife, Dianthe Lusk Brown, and two of their children. |
| Osawatomie, Kansas | • The John Brown Memorial Park, on the site of the Osawatomie battle of 1856, features a restored log cabin associated with John Brown. |

**Robert R. Potter,** educator and author, has taught on levels from junior high through graduate school. He earned an Ed.D. from Teachers College, Columbia University, in 1965, and has held professorships at both the State University of New York and the University of Connecticut. His 20 books include *Jefferson Davis: Confederate President* in the American Troublemakers series. For the past 25 years he has lived with his family in north-western Connecticut, not far from John Brown's birthplace.

**James R. Shenton** is Professor of History at Columbia University. He has taught American History since 1951. Among his publications are *Robert John Walker, a Politician from Jackson to Lincoln; An Historian's History of the United States*; and *The Melting Pot.* Professor Shenton is a consultant to the National Endowment for the Humanities and has received the Mark Van Doren and Society of Graduates' Great Teachers Awards. He also serves as a consultant for CBS, NBC, and ABC educational programs.